The Reformed Pastor

Princeton Theological Monograph Series

K. C. Hanson, General Editor

Related titles in the series

John A. Vissers
The Neo-Orthodox Theology of W. W. Bryden

Stephen Finlan and Vladimir Kharlamov, editors
Theōsis

John Thompson
The Holy Spirit in the Theology of Karl Barth

Franz Overbeck
On the Christianity of Theology

John C. Robertson Jr.
The Loss and Recovery of Transcendence

Ann Loades
Searching for Lost Coins

The Reformed Pastor
Lectures on Pastoral Theology

John Williamson Nevin

Edited by Sam Hamstra Jr.

Pickwick Publications
Eugene, Oregon

THE REFORMED PASTOR
Lectures on Pastoral Theology

Copyright © 2006 Sam Hamstra Jr. All rights reserved. Except for brief quotations in critical articles or reviews, no part of this book may be reproduced in any manner without prior written permission from the publisher. Write: Permissions, Wipf and Stock Publishers, 199 W. 8th Ave., Suite 3, Eugene, OR 97401.

Pickwick Publications
An imprint of Wipf and Stock Publishers
199 West 8th Avenue, Suite 3
Eugene, Oregon 97401

ISBN: 1-59752-383-6

Cataloging-in-Publication data

Nevin, John Williamson, 1803–1886

　　The reformed pastor : lectures on pastoral theology / edited by Sam Hamstra Jr.

　　p. ; cm

　　Princeton theological monograph series 53

　　Includes bibliographical references

　　ISBN 1-59752-383-6

　　1. Reformed Church—United States. 2. Theology—History—19th century. 3. Mercersburg theology. I. Hamstra, Sam. II. Title. III. Series.

　　BX9559 N49 2006

Manufactured in the U.S.A.

Table of Contents

Introduction by Sam Hamstra, Jr.	vii
Nevin the Pastoral Theologian	vii
Nevin's "Lectures on Pastoral Theology"	ix
Nevin the Pietist	xii
Nevin and Technique	xix
Nevin the Specialist	xxi
Conclusion	xxvi
Notes	xxvii
Lectures on Pastoral Theology by Rev. J. W. Nevin, D.D.	1
First Lecture—The Highest Office	3
Second Lecture—The Call to the Ministry	8
The Internal and External Calls	9
Pre-Requisites for Pastoral Ministry	11
Moral and Intellectual Qualifications	
for Pastoral Ministry	12

Third Lecture—Personal Holiness	15
The Necessity of Cultivating Piety	18
The Personal Benefits of Piety	22
The Practical Benefits of Piety	27
Piety and the Assurance of Salvation	30
Fourth Lecture—Evangelical Motives	36
Divine Commission	42
Sense of the Dignity of the Work	43
The Glory of God	45
Love for People	46
Confidence in the Cross	47
Attachment to Christ	48
Distinction in Heaven	49
Fifth Lecture—Fields of Labor	51
Home or Abroad	51
Financial Support	54
Preaching (First Department of Pastoral Work)	55
Matter of Preaching	55
Sixth Lecture—Manner of Preaching	57
Characteristics of Effective Preachers	57
Catechism (Second Department of Pastoral Work)	61
Visitation (Third Department of Pastoral Work)	67
Visitation of the Sick	69
Visitation of the Poor	73
Visitation of the Awakened	76
The Pastor and Relationships with Others:	78
Promotion of Peace	81
Enemies	81
Benevolent Institutions	82
Seventh Lecture—Conclusion	84
Bibliography	86

Introduction

Sam Hamstra Jr.

Nevin the Pastoral Theologian

During the relatively short history of American Protestantism, countless pastors, theologians, and pastor-theologians have addressed a variety of pragmatic issues facing Christian congregations. While many of those efforts have proven valuable to the witness and ministry of the church, for the most part, they have lacked the foundation provided by a clearly articulated ecclesiology. While the spirit of American pragmatism has produced practical works like Charles Finney's *Lectures on Revivals*, that same spirit, it seems, has discouraged thoughtful reflection on the theology that undergirds the church and its ministry. The number of American Protestants who have developed ecclesiologies built on a particular doctrinal tradition forms a short list within which John Nevin stands towards the top.

John Williamson Nevin (1803–1886) graduated from the Princeton Theological Seminary where he sat under the tutelage of Common Sense Calvinists like Archibald Alexander, Charles Hodge, and Samuel Miller. After a short term of service to the Presbyterians at their Western Theological Seminary, Nevin accepted a call from the German Reformed Church to serve as the sole professor of their seminary in the obscure village of Mercersburg, Pennsylvania. Just after his arrival in 1844, Nevin was joined by the young German church historian Philip Schaff. Together these two Idealists articulated a Christocentric system of thought that scholars have come to call "Mercersburg Theology."

The fire in John Nevin's belly was the church and its ministry. A survey of Nevin's long list of publications reveals a life dedicated to the ministry of the local congregation. Nevin made his mark in American Protestantism with the publication of *The Anxious Bench* (1843) and *The Mystical Presence* (1846). In *The Anxious Bench*, Nevin takes on Charles Finney's new measures, which had seeped their way into the life of the German Reformed Church. He denounces revivalist techniques, like altar calls and the "mourner's bench," as a hindrance to the work of the Gospel. As an alternative, Nevin promotes the "Church System" of preaching, sacraments, and catechetical instruction as the proper instrument by which the Lord, if He chooses, might send revival upon people. In *The Mystical Presence,* Nevin reaffirms and re-articulates John Calvin's insistence upon a "real, substantial, and essential" union with the incarnate and glorified Christ through the sacrament of the Lord's Supper. He clarifies his position by affirming the "spiritual real presence" of Christ in the Lord's Supper, not a local, corporeal presence.

In my lifetime, the thought of John Williamson Nevin has been examined in its historical and intellectual context for its unique contribution to the theological landscape of mid-nineteenth-century America. Scholars have gravitated, in particular, to Nevin's countercultural perspective of the church and her sacraments, to his philosophical moorings in German Idealism, and to the catholic and ecumenical spirit he shared with Philip Schaff.[1] Some of my contemporaries have employed the writings of Schaff as a resource for ecumenical dialogue, and those of Nevin as a resource for liturgical renewal. Scholars, for the most part, have stayed away from Nevin's pastoral theology.

Introduction

The reason for slighting this aspect of Nevin's thought may be that his sacramental theology represents such a monumental contribution to the historical archives of American Protestant theology that it dwarfs, by comparison, his thought in other areas. Be that as it may, Nevin's writings include many significant contributions on the role and function of the Protestant pastor in America. Nevin's pastoral theology may be viewed most clearly in five documents: a lecture called "Personal Holiness," delivered in June of 1837, at the opening of the summer term at the Western Theological Seminary; an "Inaugural Address," offered May 20, 1840, during his installation as Professor of Theology at the Theological Seminary of the German Reformed Church in Mercersburg; a sermon, delivered on July 10, 1842, entitled "The Ambassador of God: or the True Spirit of the Christian Ministry as Represented in Jesus Christ"; a sermon entitled "The Christian Ministry," delivered in 1854 for the installation service of Bernard C. Wolff (1794–1870), Nevin's successor as Professor of Theology; and the "Service of Ordination and Installation" in the Provisional Liturgy of 1857. While from different periods in his career, these documents advance a consistent viewpoint with contrasting emphases. The earlier writings emphasize the personal qualities of the pastor as the "Ambassador of God," reflecting the pietistic influence of the Puritans. The later writings deal with pastoral office and function, particularly the importance of properly installed pastors providing Christian nurture through the sacraments and catechism.

Nevin's "Lectures on Pastoral Theology"

The purpose of this volume is to provide yet one more resource from which we may gain a clearer and deeper understanding of Nevin's pastoral theology: his classroom lectures. John Nevin's "Lectures on Pastoral Theology" may be found in the excellent archives of the Evangelical and Reformed Historical Society, housed in the library of Lancaster Theological Seminary in

Lancaster, Pennsylvania. There the researcher will discover student notes from Nevin's course on pastoral theology offered during his tenure as Professor of Theology at Mercersburg Seminary (1840–1851). The archives include four sets of notes, by four different students, taken during four different semesters.[2] Nevin concluded his last course on pastoral theology just before resigning from the seminary.[3]

A careful review of the four sets of notes uncovers the learning style embraced by Nevin and his students. Nevin dictated his lectures and the students carefully recorded his every word. As a result, the student notes constitute a transcript of Nevin's lectures. Theodore Appel, one of Nevin's students and valedictorian of the class of 1850, confirms Nevin's teaching style. He writes:

> From the year 1842 to 1845, when the writer was in the Seminary, each class studied and recited from Horne's Introduction, Biblical History, with the use of Shuckford's and Prideaux's Connections, Hebrew Grammar and Bible, the Greek Testament, Jahn's Biblical Antiquities, Coleman's Christian Antiquities, Dick's Theology, Mosheim's Church History, Ernesti's Hermeneutics, and Porter's Homiletics, with lectures on Pastoral Theology.[4]

In my examination of the four sets of notes I discovered that the only measurable difference between them was punctuation. I believe we may conclude that the student lecture notes provide transcriptions of Nevin's lectures.[5]

My assumption, that the student notes constitute Nevin's "Lectures on Pastoral Theology," is further confirmed by the notes of one student, J. W. Santee. Before transcribing the third lecture, called "Personal Holiness," he notes that it was "originally delivered at the Mercersburg Theological Seminary, June, 1837, at the opening of the seminaries (sic) term - and was printed." Fortunately, that published article is extant. When I compared the four sets of student notes to that published article, I found they were nearly identical to one another.

Introduction

Nevin's "Lectures on Pastoral Theology" fall comfortably within his Christological theology. In particular, they affirm Nevin's view of the church as the body of Christ containing "objective grace in the institutions of the gospel," of the "office of the ministry as flowing from Christ's ascension," and of ordination as "investiture with a supernatural "commission."[6] In addition, Nevin's lectures contain the predictable critique of revivalist tactics. They also support his preference for the "church system" of Christian nurture, one that embraces the regular ministries of the church, including catechization and confirmation.[7]

While his lectures support the essential ingredients of his theological system, they offer silence on several issues about which Reformed Protestants might have expected a statement. Nevin does not offer the classical Reformed perspective of the sermon as the Word of God. Instead of a theological perspective on the essential nature of a sermon, he addresses the practical matter and manner of preaching. Surprisingly, while listing the functions of the pastor, Nevin does not mention the pastor's role as a liturgist. In addition, Nevin does not affirm Presbyterian polity as the biblically prescribed form of ecclesiastical government. One might even conclude from the lectures that, were he without political restraints, he might have embraced episcopal government as his preferred ecclesiastical structure. Nevin leaves the door open to such a conclusion by stating that many congregations cannot effectively call a pastor without the assistance of bishops.[8] Furthermore, he fails to distinguish the role of the pastor from that of the elders. In his lectures, Nevin does not, for example, employ the Reformed distinction between ruling and teaching elders.[9] In addition, while discussing the pastor's ministry of mercy, he fails to define how it relates to that same ministry by the diaconate.

Finally, Nevin's lectures are silent on the pastor's relationship to both the sacraments and church discipline. This silence marks a clear departure from John Calvin for whom the function of the pastor corresponded to the three marks of the true church: the preaching of the Word, the administration of the sacraments, and the exercise of church discipline. In light of the remainder of his corpus, we might excuse Nevin for not addressing the pastor's function as it relates to administrating the sacraments. From that body of literature, we know, as his students must have known, that, for Nevin, the pastor, as a representative of Christ, is privileged to administer the Lord's Supper and Baptism. But what about the pastoral function of discipline? One might speculate that, in Nevin's estimation, the pastor exercised discipline during his ministry of visitation. Yet, the absence of the word "discipline," in a pastoral theology for those in the Reformed tradition, begs for some explanation.

Those notable exceptions of silence, however, should not diminish Nevin's affirmation of several truths found within any Calvinistic theology of pastoral ministry. Nevin affirms, most notably with John Calvin, the indispensable place of the pastoral office, the pastoral office as a continuation of the apostolic office, the pastor as a representative of Jesus Christ, the necessity of both an internal and external call to the pastoral ministry, the importance of sound doctrine and holy living, and the prestige and dignity of the ordained ministry.[10] His lectures also include those general themes without which one cannot claim to be a Calvinist, including the keen awareness of the "deceitfulness of the heart," even that of the pastor, and a deep reliance and appreciation for God's providence.

Nevin's "Lectures on Pastoral Theology" represent an important addition to his published corpus for three reasons that I now look at in turn. First, through them we discover an aspect of Nevin's thought not easily discerned in other writings—the role of piety. Second, they offer a surprising confirmation of the place of technique in the ministry. Third, they offer a model of ministry that some may find appropriate for today.

Nevin the Pietist

Nevin's "Lectures on Pastoral Theology" include but a few references to his "dynamic realism" or "Romantic pursuit of the

Introduction

Ideal in the Actual."[11] They barely reflect his polemical debates over sectarianism. They do not address his deep concern over the proper use and view of the sacraments. Rather, in these lectures we find a recurring emphasis upon "the practicalities of the Christian life and less on the formal structures of theology or church order"; we find a man urging seminarians "not to rest until finding intimate fellowship with God himself."[12] In other words, these lectures reveal the pietistic side of Nevin's complex personality.

The label of "Pietist" should not startle Nevin students. While Nevin "carefully rejected the pietistic tendencies that lead to subjectivism and emotionalism, that discourage careful scholarship, and that underrate the value of Christian tradition," he publicly promoted piety.[13] In *My Own Life*, Nevin writes,

> The soul exercises of such godly men as A.H. Franke, Bengel, and Zinzendorf in Germany, the Wesleys, Whitefield, and others of like spirit in England, and in this country, belong to the inmost life of Christianity; and not to be in some sort of sympathy with them must be taken as the mark of a more or less irreligious mind. Pietism in such form has always commanded my regard, and will continue to do so always, I trust, to the end.[14]

Nevin encouraged his seminarians to have their "souls strengthened in the principles of piety." In his lecture on "Personal Holiness," he defines piety as the "power of divine life reigning within," as the "life of holiness in the soul," as "Christ dwelling deeply in the heart by faith and love," as "active fellowship with God," as "taking hold of God," and as "intimate fellowship with God himself." The systematician might properly conclude that Nevin's "piety" should be described as the process of sanctification in which the believer cooperates with the indwelling Holy Spirit. For Nevin, the believer exercises the "inward habit of piety" through prayer and faith. In prayer the Christian "takes hold of unseen things by faith." Prayer, in

Nevin's estimation, is "the opening of the mind to the light of knowledge.... It brings in the aid of God's power to guide and uphold" the Christian. In addition, it "exalts and strengthens the soul." Faith, on the other hand, "is but the education, or drawing out, of the soul itself, in its deepest capacity for knowledge."

Historian Mark Noll has identified four characteristics common to most pietistic movements: an experiential character, a biblical focus, a perfectionistic bent, and a reforming interest.[15] We find each of them in Nevin's "Lectures on Pastoral Theology."

Experience

Charles Hambrick-Stowe accurately portrays pietistic movements as a "reaction to dry scholastic rationalism in theology and hollow formalism in worship." They preach a "religion of the heart" in reaction to a "cold or formal religion that may affect the mind but never shape the morality, benevolence, and prayers of the believer."[16] Nevin echoed that pietistic thought throughout his lectures. "Religion must be a matter of personal experience and should engage the heart profoundly, no less than the understanding," wrote Nevin.[17] He encouraged seminarians with these words, "Let it sink deeply in your hearts, that the very highest and by far the most acceptable contribution of service you can render to God and his cause in the world, is comprehended in the light and power of holiness embodied and made real in your own lives."

For Nevin, the experience of personal holiness begins with conversion. Like the Puritans, Nevin feared the "calamity of the church to have unregenerate pastors."[18] He warned students that some of them may be unconverted. He boldly stated that "more ministers have been lost than have ever been saved. Hell has more of them to boast of than heaven." He invited students to seek assurance of their own conversions. "It should terrify you to think of being damned with the title of 'Reverend' upon your head." When Nevin wrote, "Save yourselves from the shipwreck of the second death," he echoed the sentiments of the Puritan, Richard Baxter, who admonished pastors with these words: "see that the work of saving grace be thoroughly wrought on your own soul."[19]

Nevin's words concerning personal experience echo those of seventeenth-century Puritanism.[20] Like the Puritans, Nevin blended his Calvinist convictions about the sovereignty of God with the human responsibility to develop the kind of personal piety that includes constant self-examination. Nevin was particularly concerned about improperly motivated ministers. He believed that the minister's public status, station in life, and opportunities for learning may attract men who substitute "official sacredness for personal religion." Hence, in his opinion, the minister must constantly question his motives to make certain he is not in the ministry for personal gain.[21]

Scripture

The second component of Nevin's pietism is biblical focus. Typically, pietists develop standards and goals from Scripture. Nevin's biblical focus, however, differs from and, in my estimation, improves upon that approach. Nevin's piety is Christological; no one would ever accuse him of "bibliolatry." Nevin lifted up Jesus Christ as revealed in the Bible. He highlighted Jesus, the Incarnate Word of God, as revealed in the written Word of God. Nevin wrote, "It is in vain for us to dream of increasing in piety, without looking to Jesus, as the author and finisher of our faith . . . It is only when he is in our eyes, that we can see clearly and impressively what we need to be; and it is only when he is before us also, that we are brought earnestly to strive after the glorious idea of a divine life." We must develop "an inward correspondence . . . with the character of Jesus Christ." We must come into "full contact with the animating and actuating mind of the Savior." We must "take the whole character of Christ for our model . . . and endeavor to be conformed to his blessed image." In short, "the piety of Jesus Christ is demanded of his followers."

Of course, those strong Christological statements cannot be divorced from Nevin's sacramental theology and Idealistic moorings. Nevin's pietism embraced private prayer and personal study, but it was also churchly and eucharistic. It was lived out of baptism and nurtured by the Lord's Supper, within the context of the church. Nor can his statements be divorced from his Reformational foundations. Nevin affirmed a Calvinistic presupposition with respect to man's ability to understand Scripture. In his estimation, without conversion, a person cannot hope to understand the Gospel. If a person has not come to faith, Nevin writes, a "portion of his understanding still slumbers within him." Consequently, he is unable to "apprehend unseen things or the realities of the spiritual world."

Perfectionism

The third component of Nevin's pietism is its perfectionistic bent, developed within a Calvinistic framework. Serious about sanctification, Nevin challenged students "to make personal holiness the great and ruling object" of their concern while preparing themselves for the ministry. They were to "be always pressing onwards in the way to perfection." As a Calvinist, however, Nevin did not expect any believer to achieve the goal of Christlikeness. He only hoped that Christians would develop a "spirit of earnestness and zeal in a religious direction" that counters the sinful human tendencies of "the spirit of party, or the thirst of praise, the pride of power, or the mere wrath of man that worketh not the righteousness of God." He encouraged seminarians towards lives that reflected "fidelity, compassion, consecration, humility, meekness, long suffering, deadness to the world, and diligence."

Nevin challenged seminarians about holy living because of his concern over the moral state of clergy. In his opinion, "the ministry has been very far from being a sanctuary of righteousness . . . to the great body of those who . . . have adventured

Introduction

upon its holy functions." Ministers "must cultivate piety to ward off the contamination of the soul by a deceitful heart." They must "come out of the world, to be separate from its maxims and fashions." If a minister fails in this endeavor, he will proudly preach himself rather than Christ. "Show me a [minister] who delights in mixed society, where he can be allowed to unbend himself from the fatigues of study, in unrestrained sympathy with the frivolous spirit of the youthful and gay around him, with only a sentimental reflection, that sounds like religion, brought in from time to time to sanctify the occasion, who by smooth gallantries wins for himself . . . . the laurels of a ladies' man, . . . and I need no prophet's inspiration to foretell that he will be neither a son of thunder nor of consolation to the church."

Reformation

The fourth component of Nevin's pietism is its reforming interest. Mark Noll writes, "Pietists usually oppose what they regard as coldness and sterility in established church forms and practices."[22] They prefer a faith that influences society. Holy living must have a public or corporate dimension. Minimally, the inward habit of piety should cultivate compassion and care for the poor.

While Nevin passed up the opportunity to offer prophetic words regarding the institution of slavery, he did express concern over the plight of the poor. For Nevin, "the relation between the poor and the rich forms a part of the Christian economy, and it does injury both to the rich and the poor if this relation is destroyed. Any church that neglects the poor cannot flourish." The pastor's role here, according to Nevin, was to mobilize the congregation to care for the poor in the community. When visiting the poor, for example, the minister should bring a gift. "The smallness of his salary should form no excuse for withholding such."

Nevin also believed that pastors should exercise political influence in the community and civic leadership. Throughout his lectures we find Nevin, the "public theologian," responding "to crises and issues in American religion and culture."[23] In his first lecture Nevin stated that "no institution is more necessary to social order and political prosperity" than the pastoral office. "It stands far above the agency of the press" with its "religious and moral influence." As a case in point, Nevin noted that nearly every college in America originated in the "hands of the ministry."

Nevin's model for social influence included the public school system, where he expected pastors to provide biblical instruction for children. Clearly, the modern understanding of the separation of church and state never entered Nevin's mind. As Richard Wenz notes, in Nevin's estimation education and religion can never be separated.[24] Nevin believed that public school "teachers are functionaries of the church."

Summary

Nevin's lectures will not lead modern scholars to dismiss their portrayals of him as a Catholic Evangelical, a Romantic Idealist,[25] or an American theologian.[26] They will, however, encourage the development of a more comprehensive portrait, one that includes a prominent place for personal piety. Specifically, these lectures will lead the contemporary reader to conclude that, while Nevin criticized revivalistic tactics, he promoted revival; that while he despised unchurchly spirituality and private interpretation, he encouraged his students to develop a dynamic and personal relationship with God; and that while he embraced the Lord's Supper as an essential means of grace, he never deprecated the significance of preaching the Gospel.

Nevin and Technique

Nevin's lectures offer a surprise for those who have studied him. It is not at all uncommon for students of Nevin to conceive of

Introduction

his criticism of new measures as the natural fruit of his Reformed heritage. As a Calvinist, when discussing the evangelistic mandate of Christ, Nevin would be expected to counter any emphasis upon human efforts or new measures with a strong statement of divine sovereignty. Interestingly, though, in his lectures Nevin does not dismiss the place of technique in the conversion process. Instead, he challenges his students to renounce the technique of "new measures," and to affirm the technique of, what we might call, "old measures," those being properly trained clergy who excel in piety and who practice the "church system." Nevin despised the "quackery" of ill-prepared and non-ordained folk parading as evangelists and, who because of their deficiencies, employed circus-like tactics in their efforts to save souls. He preferred the old-fashioned way of evangelism: ordained pastors who, while practicing piety, preach and teach the Word, trusting that God the Holy Spirit will effect conversion in the hearts of those who listen.

For Nevin, then, pastors have two reasons for developing personal piety. First, their personal relationship with Jesus Christ prompts such efforts and assures pastors of their salvation. The assurance of salvation does not appear to be a mark of salvation, as it is for modern Reformers like D. James Kennedy.[27] Instead, it seems that, from Nevin's perspective, a Reformed Christian needs continuous assurance that he or she is right with God. For Nevin, sin strips the heart of such assurance, while personal piety restores it.

Second, the pastor's effectiveness in the ministry depends upon piety. Hence, while the revivalists linked pastoral effectiveness to the proper use of techniques, Nevin linked pastoral success to the "power of divine life reigning within the soul." Even though Nevin criticized the revivalist techniques of Finney and his cohorts, he described piety as a technique essential to pastoral success. While despising new measures, Nevin did not dispense with technique. He simply replaced the anxious bench with the pastor's inward habit of piety.

In his lecture on personal holiness, Nevin wrote, "Piety is not indeed the only qualification needed to make you successful in the ministry, but it ought never to be forgotten.... No amount of advantages can make up for its absence." While the pastoral office embodies "divine power" and "carries with it objective force," the minister's piety will affect his ministry. Nevin warned students that though the office of the ministry is "invested with special force," the minister "who thinks the Spirit of the office may safely be expected to rise.... from the occasion of the office itself" is not fit for the ministry. The pastoral ministry is "stripped of its power when the pastor does not live in harmony with the mind of God." Seminarians and pastors should "study and labor systematically for the improvement of their own character . . . (The) right state of mind, relative to divine things, . . . constitutes the life and power of the sacred ministry."

For Nevin, pastoral effectiveness requires "intimate fellowship with God himself." While discussing a minister's call to the ministry, Nevin listed piety as a prerequisite and "altogether indispensable," for without it "no one can understand the Gospel." While speaking to seminarians, Nevin taught that piety is "necessary to their success as students of theology." They will never comprehend theological truth without the "medium of a spiritual mind." They must cultivate piety in order to gain knowledge. While lecturing seminarians on the demands of the ministry, Nevin stated that "the cultivation of piety is of the first consequence . . . as it respects your own comfort in the trying service to which you are devoted." "Those who give themselves to the ministry have need to make much of the power of godliness in their own souls; for without it, they are in danger of finding themselves, even in this world, of all men most miserable." While calling ministers to work at winning souls, he cites the importance of the "fire of divine love . . . stirring up . . . a holy passion for this glorious object." While discussing the power of preaching, Nevin noted that piety is the true secret of a minister's strength. The minister "speaks with authority because conviction and compassion accompany all his words." While

Introduction

describing the minister's work of pastoral visitation, Nevin stated that it "requires the deepest and most fervent piety. In the pulpit mere eloquence may help him along, but in visitation he needs more than this." Again from "Personal Holiness," we read:

> Ministers cannot serve the Gospel by the dead mechanism of human instruction. It is only as the Gospel is made to live in the soul, and utters its sound from the midst of living affections, that it becomes properly intelligible, or is made to arrest the attention of the world with its proper power. Once in a while a "carnal minister" or "dead prophet" will make a favorable impression and may even be used by God to "raise a corpse to life." But such cases are an exception. Generally, to make the Gospel felt, we must feel it ourselves. There is a deeper language necessary than that of words, to reach and move the foundations of character.

One may conclude, here, that, generally speaking, Nevin adopted the Reformed doctrine of sanctification, with its fluid relationship between the objective grace of the Holy Spirit and the subjective response of the child of God, and applied it to the relationship between the pastor and the pastoral office. Nevin wrote, "No idea can be more unreasonable, than to suppose that the ends of the Christian ministry may be answered to any extent, without an inward correspondence in him who exercises the solemn trust with it own sacred and heavenly character."[28]

Nevin the Specialist

Most historians, it seems to me, value the lessons and experiences of the past as a tutor for the present. That assumption explains my fascination with John Nevin. I am a purpose-driven pastor who needs a reason for being. When I began pastoral ministry twenty-five years ago, I discovered that neither I, nor my congregation, had a clear idea of my role. This confusion peaked when a deacon insisted that I was responsible for cutting the lawn surrounding the church building. I countered with a firm "No," but agreed to shovel the snow. Looking back, it must have been while shoveling snow one cold winter Sunday morning in Wisconsin that I decided to begin a search for a pastoral theology to support my ministry. That search led me to John Nevin.

I don't particularly resonate with Nevin's German Idealistic moorings or his liturgical convictions. I appreciate Nevin because he asked the right questions, insisted on continuity between practice and theology, and wrestled long and hard with the person and function of the pastor. I especially appreciate his pastoral theology because, with it, I finally discovered a model of ministry that makes sense both theologically and practically. For Nevin, the pastor is, first and foremost, a servant of the Word! The pastor serves the Word as a disciple of Jesus Christ, the Incarnate Word. The pastor serves the Word each Lord's Day from his pulpit through preaching, which is the Proclaimed Word. The pastor serves the Word by administrating the sacraments, the Visible Word of God.

Nevin's model of ministry helps modern pastors working within a climate of specialization and purpose-driven ministry. For Nevin, the pastor is a specialist whose purpose is to live as a servant of the Word! From the perspective of heaven, the pastor is that person called by God as an ambassador for the Incarnate Word, Jesus Christ. From the perspective of earth, the pastor is that person called by the church to represent Christ, the head of the Church, by preaching and teaching the written Word of God, the Bible. The pastor is a specialist who both knows the incarnate Word and understands the written Word. On one hand for Nevin, a pastor cannot serve the Word if he does not know the Word! For this reason, Nevin, echoing the sentiments of Puritans like Richard Baxter, emphasizes the development of the pastor's personal relationship with Jesus Christ. In one lecture, Nevin even warns his students that there are more preachers in hell than in heaven! On the other hand for Nevin, a pastor cannot serve the Word if he doesn't understand the Word. For this reason, Nevin, countering the anti-intellectual trends of his era, promoted the need for properly trained pastors with seminary training. In summary then, for Nevin, the pastor is, first and foremost, a servant of the Word.

I have discovered that viewing myself as a servant of the Word provides clarity and direction for pastoral ministry. First, Nevin's model embraces my Calvinistic heritage. Since John Calvin, a steady stream of his adherents has insisted on a theologically-trained clergy equipped to preach and teach the Word. Those who call themselves Calvinists have historically viewed the primary role of the pastor as that of preacher and teacher. Through the rite of ordination, they view pastors as under-shepherds to Jesus Christ, called by the people to represent Christ. While the pastor may be called upon to serve in a variety of capacities, he or she is, first and foremost, a servant of the Word. That conviction is affirmed by the calling practices of the Reformed community. While a pastor may accept a call to serve another congregation, the congregation usually does not have the right to sever its relationship with the pastor. The congregation understands that Christ, the chief shepherd, finally calls each pastor to serve each congregation. She understands that the pastor is finally responsible to Christ and should not be subjected to the whims of the congregation.

Second, Nevin's model promotes specialization in an age of specialization. In this respect, Nevin was ahead of his time. While he understood that, in some respects, the pastor serves as a general practitioner, he essentially developed pastors who specialized in the Word. Such an emphasis plays well in our current context, one that includes an information explosion that has, in turn, created the need for specialists who focus on limited bodies of information. The day of the general practitioner has left us. Now, nearly every field promotes specialization, including the professional ministry. Seminaries, for example, produce graduates prepared for world missions, church education, youth ministry, counseling, liturgics, and more. Right or wrong, specialization seems here to stay. Consequently, Nevin's model fits well in our culture for it encourages pastors to specialize as servants of the Word. Of course, as a specialist they may employ additional God-given gifts and, thereby, serve a variety of functions. Some pastors have the gift of leadership, for example, and may be given the opportunity to lead a local congregation. However, the pastor's fundamental role is not leader, but servant of the Word. One who does not serve the Word, may be a minister of one type or another, but he or she is not a pastor.

Third, Nevin's model anchors the pastor when the winds of faddish trends sweep through the church. Several fads have come and gone, including the pastor as evangelist, the pastor as counselor, the pastor as physician of the soul, the pastor as servant leader, and the pastor as CEO.[29] Each fad, it seems to me, represents more the influence of culture than that of the Spirit in a church that is always reforming. I am especially concerned about the most recent fad, which has deeply influenced the life of the American Protestant church: the pastor as political leader.[30] I distinguish that kind of leadership from the spiritual leadership that pastors naturally bring to their ministries as representatives of Christ and models of Christian devotion. A personal survey of recent works on pastoral ministry reveals disturbing consensus regarding the role of the pastor. Several authors, without scriptural or theological rationale, propose that pastors are necessarily political leaders. This fad has confused many pastors and hindered the ministries of many congregations. Some pastors without the gift of leadership despairingly question their fitness for ministry as servants of the Word. Other pastors without the gift of leadership exercise what they think is leadership to the demise of their congregations. I write as a pastor with the gift of political leadership. God has placed me in settings where that gift has been desired by the congregations I have served. However, there are many congregations that do not require pastors with the gift of leadership; God has equipped them with leadership through other gifted individuals. These congregations are faithfully and admirably served by pastors without the gift

Introduction

of political leadership. These same pastors bring a different gift-mix to their ministries, but remain fundamentally servants of the Word. In that capacity, they provide spiritual leadership as they represent Christ and model Christian discipleship.

Fourth, Nevin's model provides direction for pastors questioning the application of ordination. Living before the days of specialized ministry, Nevin did not imagine a time when theologically-trained individuals would serve in a capacity outside of the pastorate. In his day, only seminary trained individuals, called by God to serve as pastors, received the rite of ordination as Ministers of the Word and Sacraments. Times have changed. Specialization has arrived and benefited local congregations and the ministry of Christ throughout the world. However, as a result of specialized ministry, and its correlate specialized educational training, local congregations often face difficult decisions about who to ordain as Ministers of the Word and Sacraments. In my circle, the current practice, though not officially articulated, suggests that the church ordain any person with a Master of Divinity degree from a seminary serving in some kind of people-helping or educational position. My denominational directory of ordained ministers includes school principals, social workers, therapists, professors, administrators, fund-raisers, and pastors. I suggest that Nevin's model offers an excellent guideline for the church as it seeks to determine appropriate candidates for ordination. I believe that those who serve the Incarnate and living Word, Jesus Christ, and serve the written Word through study and proclamation, should be ordained. I encourage the church to ordain, as it has in the past, pastors of local congregations whose primary responsibilities include the proclamation of the Word. I also encourage the ordination as Ministers of the Word and Sacraments for professors of theology and chaplains. However, I discourage ordination or the retention of ordination for those called to important vocations within which their primary responsibilities do not include studying and proclaiming the Word. I include in this group therapists, school administrators, denominational bureaucrats, para-church administrators, and social workers.[31] I would hope that ordination as a Minister of the Word and Sacraments would say to the church and to the world, "This person is a servant of the Word."

Conclusion

Before the reader proceeds to Nevin's lectures, I offer a handful of warnings or disclaimers. First, like most Christians in the nineteenth century outside of the burgeoning charismatic movement, Nevin assumed that the pastoral office was for men and his lectures reflect that conviction. I follow Nevin's lead and do not attempt to counter his exclusivity. I hope that pastors of both genders will not interpret this decision as promoting a position regarding pastors who happen to be women. Second, the reader should know that, while I use the term *pastor* to refer to the person who holds the office of the "Ministry of the Word and Sacraments," Nevin uses the words *pastor* and *minister* synonymously, and employs the latter term far more frequently than the former. Third, in my study of the four versions of student notes, I have discovered the fountain-ink-pen handwriting of J.W. Santee easiest to read. My quotes come from his copy. Fourth, Nevin's students employed a couple different tools as points of emphasis, including the under-lining of words and the capitalization of the first letter of key words. Remarkably, I discovered that the students often underlined the same words. However, they did not employ upper case letters in a consistent manner. I chose to italicize the words underlined by students, and to use lower case letters with nearly all words within sentences. In so doing, I recognize that, in other writings, Nevin often capitalized words like church, and providence.

Finally, I offer a word of gratitude to the excellent staff of the Evangelical and Reformed Historical Society, whose offices and archives are located in the Philip Schaff Library of the Lancaster Theological Seminary in Lancaster, Pennsylvania. The Society, by providing excellent archives and by granting permission to

Introduction

publish Nevin's lectures, has fulfilled its purpose to stimulate and cultivate interest in the heritage of the Reformed Church in the United States.

Notes

[1] *Reformed Confessionalism in Nineteenth-Century America: Essays on the Though of John Williamson Nevin*, edited by Sam Hamstra, Jr., and Arie J. Griffioen (Scarecrow, 1995).
[2] E.W. Reinecke (Winter Session 1845–1846), Geo. Wolff (May 1847), J. B. Thompson (Winter Session 1847–1848), and J. W. Santee (July 1850).
[3] One measurement of Nevin's influence through his students is class enrollment. While the Mercersburg Seminary class of 1842 included nineteen students, only ten members were in attendance in 1851. Most classes during Nevin's tenure did not exceed 13 students. See George Warren Richard's *History of the Theological Seminary of the Evangelical and Reformed Church at Lancaster, Pennsylvania* (Lancaster, Pa.: Rudisill and Company, 1952).
[4] *Life and Work of John Williamson Nevin*, by Theodore Appel (Philadelphia: Reformed Church Publication House, 1889) 418.
[5] Since I view the student notes of Nevin's "Lectures on Pastoral Theology" as faithful representations of Nevin's thought, when quoting from a student's notes, I have ascribed the words to John Nevin and placed them within quotation marks.
[6] John Williamson Nevin, "Vindication of the Revised Liturgy," *The Living Theological Heritage of the United Church of Christ*, edited by Charles Hambrick-Stowe (Cleveland: Pilgrim, 1998) III: 492.
[7] Like the Puritans, Nevin believed that the pastor was, in some respects, a physician of the soul. "Ministers are shepherds, employed to watch over the flock of Christ," he wrote. "A pastor must know his congregation to such a degree that he discovers each congregant's spiritual condition and responds accordingly." Towards the fulfillment of that goal, Nevin echoed the Puritans insistence upon catechizing the youth and personal instruction in the home as essential pastoral duties.
[8] In unpublished student notes of his "Lectures on Didactic Theology," Nevin identifies four types of church government: popery, episcopal, presbyterian, and independent. He then identifies presbyterian government as that "form in which the official power is handed down in succession." He continues with a comparison to episcopacy, stating that Presbyterianism affirms the parity of congregations and clergy, embraces a system of representative government that is not a democracy because the ministry is a standing office, not the creation of men, and divides the presbyters into teaching and ruling elders, supported by deacons who have charge of "temporalites." See the student notes by J. B. Thompson, of Nevin's 1847 seminary course on Didactic Theology, in the archives of the Evangelical and Reformed Historical Society, housed in the library of Lancaster Theological Seminary in Lancaster, Pennsylvania.
[9] Heinrich Heppe, *Reformed Dogmatics*, Revised and edited by Ernst Bizer, Translated by G. T. Thomson (Grand Rapids: Baker, 1978): XXVII.39.
[10] John Calvin, *Institutes of the Christian Religion*, IV.3.1-16.
[11] William DiPuccio, "The Dynamic Realism of Mercersburg Theology: The Romantic Pursuit of the Ideal in the Actual" (Ph.D. dissertation, Marquette University, 1994).

[12] Mark Noll on "Pietism" in *Evangelical Dictionary of Theology*, edited by Walter Elwell (Grand Rapids: Baker, 1984).
[13] George W. Richard, *History of the Theological Seminary*, 271.
[14] John W. Nevin, "My Own Life," *Reformed Church Messenger*, June 8, 1870.
[15] Mark Noll lists four characteristics of "Pietism" may be found in the *Evangelical Dictionary of Theology*, edited by Walter Elwell (Grand Rapids: Baker, 1984).
[16] Charles Hambrick-Stowe, editor, *The Living Theological Heritage of the United Church of Christ* (Cleveland: Pilgrim, 1998) III: 312–13.
[17] John W. Nevin, "My Own Life," *Reformed Church Messenger*, June 8, 1870.
[18] Richard Baxter, *The Reformed Pastor* (London: Epworth, 1939) 156, 163.
[19] Richard Baxter, *The Reformed Pastor*, 156.
[20] Samuel T. Logan, "Puritanism" in the *Dictionary of the Presbyterian and Reformed Tradition in America*, edited by D.G. Hart (Downers Grove, Ill.: InterVarsity, 1999) 203–205.
[21] The Puritans and Nevin recommended similar motives for those serving as pastors. This affinity may be discovered by comparing Nevin's convictions about pastoral motives to those of the Baxter. Both specify the necessity of a commission by God and the obligation to respond to that call, the realization of the honor of the position in that a pastor is a steward of God's own family, and the deep appreciation for the price paid for the church, that being the blood of Jesus Christ.
[22] Noll, "Pietism."
[23] Richard Wentz, *John Williamson Nevin: American Theologian* (New York: Oxford University Press, 1997) 11.
[24] Richard Wentz, *John Williamson Nevin: American Theologian*, 29.
[25] See James Hastings Nichols, *Romanticism in American Theology* (Chicago: The University of Chicago Press, 1961).
[26] See Richard Wentz, *John Williamson Nevin: American Theologian*.
[27] See *Evangelism Explosion*, by D. James Kennedy (Wheaton, Ill.: Tyndale, 1972).
[28] Nevin's student, Emanuel V. Gerhart, the systematician of Mercersburg Theology, echoed the thoughts of his mentor: "the success of (the pastor's) labors depends entirely upon the degree of his faith and piety . . . but not on the divine powers of his office, nor on his authority to administer the sacraments, and to remit or retain sin the sense of Christ's words. Excerpted by J. H. Good in "Are Ministers of the Gospel Priests and Kings?", *Reformed Church Monthly* (February 1868), reprinted in *The Living Theological Heritage of the United Church of Christ*, edited by Elizabeth C. Nordbeck and Lowell H. Zuck (Cleveland: Pilgrim, 1998) IV:577.
[29] See the pastor as CEO in George Barna, *Marketing the Church: What They Never Taught You about Church Growth* (Colorado Springs: Navpress, 1988).
[30] For example, see how the words "pastor" and "leader" are used synonymously in William H. Willimon, *Pastor: The Theology and Practice of Ordained Ministry* (Nashville, Tenn.: Abingdon, 2002).
[31] My conviction should not be understood as an attack on the professions just listed. God has called many individuals to such vocations. In fact, I once served as a vice-president for advancement in a Christian college, but do not believe I should have retained my ordination as a Minister of the Word and Sacraments. Also, I encourage Reformed Christians to recognize that the practice of ordaining individuals who are not servants of the Word counters the teaching of the priesthood of all believer and that of vocation. In the end, the practice creates a class system within the church with the ordained holding a higher rank over the non-ordained.

Lectures on
Pastoral Theology

Rev. John W. Nevin, D.D.

Lecture One

The Highest Office

The highest office with which it is possible for a man to be invested in this world is that of the *Christian ministry*. No one can hesitate to admit this, who believes the Gospel to be true, and reflects seriously on the origin and nature of the office, its relations and bearings as they are presented to our view.

The main design of the ministry is the edification of the church. This may be said to comprehend in a certain sense all that is important in the history of the world. In the midst of the universal desolation which has been created on earth by sin, God has undertaken to erect for himself a new spiritual creation: a kingdom of light and glory, having its seat in the character of its subjects, by which the empire of darkness is finally to be overthrown, even in this world; and which is destined to endure with glory, honor, and immortality, world without end, when the earth and heavens shall be no more. In this interest is comprised, of course, all the hope of the human race. Apart from it the affairs of the world have no significance or value. From the beginning down to the present hour, the great system of Providence has been administered with steady reference to it as the soul of all that belongs to man's history or destination.

To serve the great design, Jesus Christ, in the fullness of time, assumed our nature, carried our griefs and sorrows in the days of his flesh, and poured out his life finally upon the cross, to make expiation for our sins, and to reconcile us to God. In the fulfilment of the same work, he rose from the dead, ascended on high, leading captivity captive, and took his mediatorial place in the heavens; where he ever liveth to make intercession for all that draw nigh to God in his name; and from whence he carried forward the government of the world, solemnly laid upon his shoulders, in full and complete subservience to the interests of the church, till the end shall come. For the accomplishment of his work, he gave the church an outward and visible form, and established a peculiar system of ordinances and powers, in the proper use of which it should be advanced continually more and more in its own life, and extended in its limits, until at last it might become universally triumphant. Among those arrangements the ministry holds a prominent place. It forms, we may say, the life and soul of the entire system. Here a particular class of men, divinely designated for the purpose, is set apart from the bosom of the general church, age after age, to preside with special authority over its spiritual interests, and to carry forward in its behalf the counsels of the Master's mind for the attainment of the great ends for which it has been instituted. Under every view in which such an office can be contemplated, its importance must appear truly vast and solemn.

Not only is it of divine appointment, but it has the character of a commission from Christ to act directly under his authority and in his name. This appears from the names which are applied to ministers in the Bible, and also from the terms in which their office is described. They are called "stewards." "Let a man so account of us as of the ministers of Christ, and *stewards* of the mysteries of God." With this, the Apostle intends to induce in them a sense of their high responsibilities. They are called *Ambassadors*. "Now then we are *Ambassadors* for Christ, as though

Lecture One

God did beseech you by us; we pray you in Christ's stead, be ye reconciled to God." Christ is the *Chief Shepherd*, and ministers are shepherds under him, employed to watch over the flock. They are *sent* forth by Christ. "As my father hath sent me, even so send I you." When he ascended on high, he led captivity captive and gave gifts unto men. And he gave some apostles, and some prophets, and some evangelists, and some pastors and teachers, for the perfecting of the saints, the work of the ministry, for the edifying of the body of Christ. It is employed in the highest concerns. Christ represents them in the Gospel as standing in the same relation to him, as he to the Father. Ministers are appointed to teach the divine will—to dispense the mysteries of the kingdom of heaven—to labor for the salvation of the *soul*. No mere temporal interests. They must make prayer—dispense the sacraments—visit the sick—be present at death. The office is invested with special force and virtue for its own ends. As a divine institution, it embodies divine power.

Even in a temporal point of view it is of immense account. No institution is more necessary to social order and political prosperity. It stands far above the agency of the press in a Christian land. It is a religious and moral influence, and hence goes beyond any other. Legislation does not reach us so far as the pulpit. There never has been an agency instituted so extensive as this. The ministry also stands linked with all secular interests. The world owes much to it, as it respects learning. Refer to the Middle Ages. Witness all the present time. Almost all our important institutions of learning have grown out of its interests. The conduct of these colleges has almost invariably been in the hands of the ministry. The deviation from this rule has never been found to work well.

This forms, however, the lowest aspect that can be taken. Its importance lies especially in its relation to eternity. It is a divine institution, and as such must be considered as embodying a divine power. As such it must also be considered as carrying with it an objective force or power. "Not even in the light of the sun," says Calvin, "not even is meat and drink so necessary for the support and cherishing of life, as is the maintenance and support of the ministry of the Gospel church on earth." Well might the apostle spake of it as a *good* work. It is so if we look at its origin, at the qualifications it requires, at the excellency of the Christian dispensation, at its design and nature, at its suitableness to improve those who attend on it, in virtue and knowledge, at its rewards, here and hereafter. No office is so honorable and high.

All this rightly considered will produce *humility* in ministers themselves. There is no danger of estimating too highly the dignity of the office. Paul says, "Not a novice, lest being lifted up with pride he fall into the condemnation of the devil." He should not be inflated with the view that the world is supposed to take of it. This will also produce a sense of *responsibility*, and an anxiety to be found faithful. Men may have some sense of responsibility, as they may have in a civil office: but ministers should have a higher sense than this, and hence they should contemplate the great responsibility of a *divine institution*. This will induce faithfulness in the discharge of its functions. Faithfulness is the first requisite of a steward. This sense of responsibility should accompany us in preparing for the office, in discharging and fulfilling its duties. Another effect of a right view of the ministry will be contempt of worldly honor, wealth and ease. In proportion as men look upon it as a secular interest, they will have more respect to their ease and worldly involvement. But we ought to be lifted up above this feeling. We should stand above all worldly interests. Again, attachment to the work and entire consecration. Under a worldly view it is invested with a high honor. Young men often look to it in this respect. But when men come to be invested with the office itself, a change frequently takes place. The romance of the thing has passed away. The true interest and dignity lies not in its worldly estate but in its spiritual dignity and interest, and these are to be apprehended by faith. If a man has not a proper apprehension of his office as being spiritual, its dignity will sink deeply in his own eyes. Hence, Paul says, "I magnify my office." The man needs to fix

Lecture One

his eyes on the source of the ministry as a divine institution. Hence it is a great thing to magnify the office as Paul did, not only theoretically, but actually in feeling. This may be a criterion to our minds of true faith. The want of this, proceeds from unbelief and worldliness. Again: thankfulness to God for being called to so high a work. We see this strikingly exhibited in the case of Paul. He seems sometimes to set it above his conversion.

Lecture Two

Call to the Ministry

What constitutes a call to the ministry? As the sacred office is of divine institution, so there must be a divine *call*, in every case to bring men into it, and clothe them with its authority. If any one should question the necessity of such a call, there must be a suspicion that a proper conception of the office, its origin and bearings, is wanting.

The necessity for such a call appears from the nature of the case, as already set forth, from the names applied to those invested with the office. They are called ambassadors. They must be appointed by a person whom they represent in virtue of whose appointment they are ambassadors, not self constituted, but in the name of the master of the household, watchmen, ministers. All these names setting forth the different sides of the same office preclude self-constitution and demand a call from the source of authority. They are only so far anything as they work in virtue of him whom they represent, says the apostle.

> *Who then is Paul? And who is Apollos but ministers by whom ye believe, even as the Lord gave to every*

Lecture Two

> *man. I have planted, Apollos watered, but God gave the increase. So there is neither he that planteth anything, neither he that watereth but the Lord that gave the increase. (I Corinthians 3:5-6)*

All are bound to serve one another in the church but a peculiar order has been set apart for the regular and public work of the ministry. We must not, however, look upon it, as holding an abstract position to the church, but as flowing out of the church. Notwithstanding, it is of divine appointment, and no one, not of this order, has a right to direct and teach the church, in a public way. No one is at liberty to take the office for himself. God *only* can call. "How shall they preach except they be sent." So with the priesthood. "No one taketh this honor to himself, but he that is called of God." This passage has reference to Christ, but also to ministers as standing in the same relation to God. So in the beginning, God appointed the extraordinary ministers, prophets, and apostles, etc. and endowed them with gifts. Paul speaks of himself as an apostle of God, not of men.

This call may be *extraordinary and ordinary*. The first classed with inspiration and miraculous gifts. The apostles were extraordinary officers, and various others were raised for extraordinary offices and furnished with extraordinary gifts. The ordinary call is that with which we have to do. It is *internal and external*. The call to be complete must include both. The *external* call consists of a commission received from the church by means of a regularly constituted ecclesiastical authority already established in her bosom. Our view of this call will depend in some measure upon our view of the church. If we restrict the church, we will of course, limit the call. The call is regular when it proceeds from the proper authorities in the church. The ministry springs from and stands rooted in the general life of the church. If we look upon it as holding an abstract position with regard to, and not a living relation to the church, it becomes hierarchic.

This call is not complete, and cannot of itself qualify a man for the work. It only communicates official authority and gives validity to ministerial acts. It may even form the channel of spiritual blessing. Yet this cannot have its proper form without the internal. It supposes an internal call, but it cannot generate it. It may have place where no such call has gone before. Still it forms a part of the divine call itself, in all ordinary cases.

The external call stands in the same relation to the internal as baptism to regeneration. Thus the external call must not be looked upon as a mere human appointment. It is the proper externalization of the internal call: that by which the latter is ratified. It is not a mere appointment, as that of the offices of societies. The ordination carries with it a *sacramental force*. Hence the Catholic church has made it a full sacrament. This sacramental character is peculiar to the church. But we must here guard against the other extreme, and make it equal with the other sacraments. A great deal of controversy about the sacraments is mere (logomachy). In the church the authority which invests [a person] with office is from God and acts for God.

The *internal* call is necessary as the ground of the other. So the church has always thought. This call however, is not miraculous, by inspiration, or a sign from heaven. The church is the judge of it. Men have no reason to expect a special dispensation supernaturally. It lies in the direction of God's grace and providence. Mere *piety* does not constitute a call to the ministry for piety belongs to the whole church. Nor the designation of parents and friends. This has obtained in the English church. Yet we must not undervalue this call. We have cases of this kind of designation in the Old Testament. The pains of the parents in educating their children may produce the qualifications. No more impropriety in this than in designating a child in baptism and educating him to be a Christian. Yet mere education does not make out the call. A simple inclination does not constitute a call. Serious and prayerful examination are necessary to settle the point. No question can be more entitled to such examination. Every one should tremble at the thought of entering such an office, without the call. For the true minister, it is of the highest importance that he should be well assured of and live in the

Lecture Two

habitual consciousness of his call. This is necessary for comfort, patience, resolution, and vigor in his work. Hence the importance of settling our call, not only that we may not fall in the condemnation of the unseen, but be properly encouraged.

Three things are necessary. Where an individual finds himself. 1. Possessed of the requisite qualifications. 2. Is urged with a strong and steady desire for the work. 3. Has the way been thrown open for his introduction to it in divine providence, he may consider himself divinely called.

1. The requisite qualifications are piety and aptness or capacity to teach. Piety is altogether indispensable and forms the very element. Without this no one can understand the Gospel. How then teach it to others? God calls no unconverted person. Piety alone is not sufficient, yet it must not be wanting. Much more, it should be marked clear and evident. He ought to go before others—be a pattern and example of piety. Aptness to teach is required expressly. "Faithful men, who may be able to teach others also." There may be a defect of voice: if this is insurmountable, it alone is sufficient evidence that he is not called. Mental simplicity, of course, constitutes a more serious objection still, for he must teach. Prevailing ignorance, through want of education, forms a proper objection at the time. He may prepare himself and then be called.
2. In case of a true *call*, a *desire* for the work is produced in the mind by the Spirit of God. "This is a true saying, if a man desires the office of a Bishop, he desireth a good work."
    a. This desire should be constraining, something more than the general desire of promoting God's glory which every Christian is supposed to have. The Prophet speaks of it as a "fire in the bones." "Woe to me," says Paul, "If I preach not the Gospel." Other employments seem poor in comparison. The idea of any other work, strips life of its interest.

b. The desire should be *considerate*. Not a fit of zeal, momentary and fickle. Not a party purpose. New converts frequently have such a momentary desire, but it soon passes away. The cost must be counted, the nature of the office considered. The desire must remain as a fixed habit.
c. The desire must be *disinterested*, terminating on the work itself. Here the deceitfulness of the hearts shows itself, and sometimes shows itself very strongly. There are powerful inducements to engage in the work of the ministry. A man may desire to be in the ministry for his own end, to make a living, to have credit and standing, to make himself felt in the world, to enjoy literary ease, or even to promote his own salvation. All these motives are wrong. A man may have the desire of a still higher kind. The welfare of the race. Yet this is not sufficient. Our desire to be right, must be to serve the end of the ministry itself.
3. The way must be thrown open in the providence of God. This implies that the individual may have the opportunity of securing an education and then have an external opportunity of entering. If he cannot have a proper education, if he cannot separate himself from other duties without violence, it is plain that he is not called. Sometimes these obstructions may be intended to try his faith. And if all other obstructions are away, and he cannot get the proper ecclesiastical introduction, he is not called. No one has a right to preach on his own authority.

Qualifications for the Ministry are Intellectual and Moral

1. Intellectual
a. *Natural Talent*. A weak man, though pious, should not get into such an office. It is a waste of time and toil to bring forward such. Want of such can only do harm. Not high

and sublime talents, but discretion, prudence. Beware of helping to bring forward persons incompetent in this respect.

b. *Learning*. To teach we must be taught either in an extraordinary way or ordinary one. The Apostles had no learning, yet were extraordinarily taught. The minister should have his power disciplined. He needs also wide resources. He is to teach, and is set for the defense of the truth against infidels and heretics. The apostles were three years with Christ, and then miraculously gifted. We should aim at a learned ministry. There is a temptation constantly to become lax in this matter. Because the field is white for the harvest, and laborers few, men are led to undervalue learning. The want is great, yet it is a proper ministry, not of an unlearned but of a learned ministry. What good can an unlearned man do in the ministry, that he might not do out of it? They can still be teachers in Sunday School. Tract distributors. We have sufficient unlearned ministers and the want does not lie here. There always will be enough of unlearned ministers at any rate, and we need not take any pains to multiply them. Every new sect generally, goes on the principle that the world is to be converted by an unlearned ministry. The great, real, true want is the want of a learned ministry. The very fact that there are such sects, makes it necessary that the regular denominations should have a learned ministry. The regular ministry forms a regular force. To keep up a tolerable number of learned ministers, a general rule is needed, a measure to which all should endeavor to attain. New systems of education should not be tried. The old is still to be preferred as tried by experience, languages, mathematics, etc. Discipline is the main thing. We have no reason to object to the usual course. All knowledge should be taught in its place. All enlarges and improves the mind.

c. *Eloquence or ability to speak*. He should be able to speak clearly and distinctly. Defect in voice may be an evidence that a man is not called, the great requisite to speak well is first to *understand*, and then to *feel* our subject.

2. Moral Qualifications

Piety in an eminent degree; for his own comfort that he may be faithful, eloquent, may avoid error and sin (from which otherwise he can never be secure), must find a satisfying interest in his work, that he may lead others in the right way as a teacher generally; that he may prove a large reward in the end. This includes *zeal, fidelity* (this tries his integrity; his work is a trust), *compassion* towards men—*entire consecration*, humility, meekness, long suffering—deadness to the world, temperate in all things, habitual diligence—anxiety for souls, and solicitude for the result of his labors—learning to prayer, etc. Paul's third chapter to Timothy, and Epistle to Titus should be read seriously with reference to this end.

Lecture Three
Personal Holiness

Introduction

I propose, in this lecture, my dear young friends, to urge upon you once more the great duty of cultivating *personal holiness* in the midst of your other preparations for the work of the sacred ministry. It is not necessary that I should offer any apology for doing this, on the present or on any other occasion; though the subject may be considered so plain and trite a character, as hardly to authorize the expectation of any thing being said upon it, with which you are not in one sense already perfectly familiar. It has been solemnly imposed as a duty on your instructors, by the church from which they hold their office, to admonish and exhort you with regard to this interest continually; and they would be deserving of pity, indeed, if, independently of all such obligation, they were not prompted by their own hearts to consult for your spiritual improvement, more earnestly than for any other advantage they can desire on your behalf. We appreciate the value of knowledge, and are concerned that you should be diligent in improving every opportunity you enjoy, for acquiring it, under all its forms. We would not diminish, in the slightest degree, your ardor in the prosecution of your studies, or in the cultivation of such natural resources as God may have blessed you with, for becoming skillful theologians or popular preachers. On the contrary, we should be glad if your zeal and activity in this direction were greatly increased; and we are fully persuaded, that by growing in piety you cannot fail to become always more conscientiously strict and earnest in your character as students. The power of a divine life, reigning within you can never dispose you to neglect your studies, or to use with a slack hand the means you possess for making your education for the ministry thorough and complete. It is not when led by the Spirit of God, that the theological student is found out of place and out of time, as it respects the literary engagements to which he is bound in an institution like ours; slighting his lessons, absenting himself from recitations, despising rules, careless of punctuality, wasting his time with unprofitable visits, and sacrificing his intellectual strength to the vain spirit of the world. We would not lend the smallest countenance to the thought, that you may safely neglect your studies. They are entitled to more than all the zeal they have yet received at your hands. But still, the interest to which your attention is now called, we are bound to regard as unspeakably above every other that you are required to consider. It is too momentous, indeed, to be weighed at all with any other advantage that may be desirable in your circumstances; for it is the presence of piety alone that can impart any true value to all other training for the sacred office. The ministry of reconciliation, though clothed with every accomplishment of learning and eloquence, is shorn of its glory and emptied of its power just so soon and so far as the spirit of holiness is found wanting to its solemn offices.

The simplest idea we can form of holiness, as it concerns ourselves, is derived from the character and life of Jesus Christ. One great object of his appearing in our nature was, that the mind of God might be brought within our reach, and rendered intelligible to us, by clothing itself with the conditions and attributes of humanity. To be holy is to be in harmony with the mind of God; and the character of Christ accordingly stands before us as the fullest possible revelation we can have of what we should aim at in our endeavors to attain to this blessed distinction. Hence it is in vain for us to dream of increasing in piety without "looking to Jesus, the author and finisher of our faith," in this respect. It is only when he is in our eyes, that we can see clearly and impressively what we need to be; and it is only when he is before us also, that we are brought earnestly to strive after the glorious idea of a divine life, so as to realize the power of it in any degree by growing in grace. His example instructs and captivates at the same time. We behold, so as at once to understand and admire, and in seeing the righteousness we are called to make our own, the glory and honor of it are so discovered also, as to become to our souls the post powerful of all attractions, drawing us to Christ and away from all our sins.

This is the true secret of Christian sanctification. We do but deceive our own hearts, when we talk of cultivating religion in any other way, or fancy that we are growing in grace without this sort of distinct inward correspondence kept up in our minds with the character of Jesus Christ. And it is not enough here, that the example of Christ should be referred to in a merely speculative way, to recommend or enforce certain moral duties, such as patience, humility, meekness, and etc., as these may commend themselves to respect in a simply human point of view. What we need is to come into full contact with the animating and actuating mind of the Savior; to understand and feel the meaning of his character, in the light of its own living relations and divine principles, as the gloriously perfect idea of holiness in our fallen nature. It is only when we come to look at Christ in this way, and begin to apprehend that the spirit of his life, consisting in a holy sympathy and moral oneness with the mind of the infinite Jehovah himself, is the very righteousness to which we also are called, that we can be said to have entered on the process of "proving what is that good, and acceptable, and perfect will of God," which constitutes the true salvation of the gospel. We can have no evidence that we are in earnest in following after holiness, until we are brought to take the whole character of Christ for our model, and are conscious of actively desiring and distinctly endeavoring to be conformed to his blessed image, that is, to have wrought in us by the mighty power of God, the very mind that induced him to appear in the flesh, ran through all his life and ministry, and shone most affectingly at the last through his sorrows on the cross. The piety of Jesus Christ was the same with the piety that is demanded of his followers. "If any man serve me," so runs his own solemn declaration, "let him follow me"—let him be like me, enter into my spirit, mold himself inwardly into my mind, and walk in my steps.

What conception of Christianity can we have more simple and clear and full! Happy were if for the church, it were more in the minds of those who bear the Christian name. When I exhort you to the cultivation of piety, it is to this lofty style of character I desire to direct your thoughts. You are more by profession than ordinary followers of Christ; you are aspiring to go before others, as guides and examples to the flock. How does it become you, then, to keep close to his steps in your souls, and to make personal holiness the great and ruling object of your concern, in all you are now doing to prepare yourselves for the ministry.

I. The Cultivation of Religion in Your Own Hearts Is Necessary to Your Success as Students of Theology

You are in the habit of admitting, no doubt, that there can be no right knowledge of divine things, without some experience of the power of them in your soul. But this admission is often made, without a sufficiently deep and clear impression of the extent of that general truth which has now been stated. To understand it properly, and to feel the practical force of it as we should, we need to resolve it in our thoughts more frequently and earnestly than is commonly done. Superficial thoughts here are not enough.

Lecture Three

Nothing can be more reasonable, where the efficacy of prayer is admitted at all, than to believe that the diligent use of it for the purpose, will ensure divine aid in the prosecution of knowledge as really as in any other laudable pursuit. Solomon asked wisdom of God, and it was given him in extraordinary measure; not independently of his own studies, but by divine help going along with those studies, in a way incomprehensible to men, but with an agency as real as that which he employed afterwards in marshaling the clouds of heaven and causing them to pour down rain in answer to the prayers of Elijah. Why should it be so? Does he not hold in his hand the spirits of men as truly as all the fountains of change in the outward world, and can he not order the course of nature, according to his own pleasure, as truly in the one case as in the other? If we may look for divine interpositions in our behalf, when we call upon God, where other blessings dependent on the course of events around us are concerned, it cannot be fanatical surely to look for them also for the direction and support of our own powers, when we pray for his blessing on our studies. How innumerable are the conditions necessary to constitute, in our case, the best state and frame of mind for study, which it is impossible for us for the most part fully to understand beforehand, but which are all open to the knowledge of our Maker, and entirely within the compass of his disposing providence! Shall we say, that prayer may not avail, far beyond the light of our own discretion and the prudence of friends, to secure a favorable ordering of these in our behalf? And who will doubt, but that God, who beholds always and always sustains in action, the mysterious mechanism of our minds, may operate within them, to a most important extent, to facilitate and crown with success their endeavors after knowledge? And shall we not labor to bring into our studies, then, this co-operating power of heaven; that reason, and memory, and imagination, as well as all our moral affections, may be refined, and invigorated, and conducted to the best results, by its quickening presence?

But the maxim, *Bene orasse est bene studuisse*,[1] carries with it a

---
[1] "To have prayed well is to have studied well."

still deeper sense than this. It implies that prayer is itself the opening of the mind to the light of knowledge. It is of interest to the student, not merely as it brings in the foreign aid of God's power to guide and uphold his studies in other ways, secret and inexplicable to all but God himself; but in a more immediate and still more interesting way, as it does by its own nature exalt and strengthen the soul, and usher it into the region of truth, so as to carry in itself most wonderfully the blessing it is intended to secure. And in this respect all prayer, as well as that which more immediately respects this end, falls in harmoniously with the true idea of study, and works actively with it in favor of knowledge; which is but to say, in other words, that the power of a divine life in the soul, whose great constituent is the spirit of prayer taking hold of unseen things by faith, forms at once the best disposition, and the strongest support, and the surest impulse, with regard to knowledge, which the powers of the human mind can ever be brought to receive.

Faith, in the sense of the Scriptures, is the most active and comprehensive of all the faculties that enter into the structure of the understanding. It is the crowning power of intelligence; inasmuch as all other forms of knowledge are but the scaffolding by which the mind is raised towards this, and as without this it can never be said to have reached the true and full development of its own nature. Faith is not a foreign element super-added to the original constitution of the soul; it is but the education, or drawing out, of the soul itself, in its deepest capacity for knowledge. It constitutes the very perfection of rationality, the clearest and most active exercise of intellect. The mind in which it is wanting, is a defective mind. It has never yet reached its full and proper physical development. This development, however, is nothing more nor less than the inward habit of piety. We may see at once, then, how far from the truth is the supposition cherished by some, that religion has little or nothing to do with knowledge. It involves the highest order of education for the mind, in its very nature.

If the statement just made be true, it is evident that the spirit of piety is of the greatest account, in the case of every kind of study, whether it relate to divine things or not. In one sense, all the objects of knowledge are divine things. They may be considered apart from God, but still their most important aspects and relations grow out of their connection with Him, as the author of all the order and design that belongs to them, and the everywhere present and all-glorious *Life,* the sense of which in the mind is alone sufficient to bring any inquirer into contact with their true significance. The man whose intelligence, in the form of faith, has never yet apprehended unseen things, the realities of that spiritual world to which all that is seen stands related only as a shadow to the substance it represents, is not prepared to enter far into the meaning of that world of facts with which he is surrounded in the body. He occupies a false position for observation. The true center of that system of things which is before him is not in his eye; and of course all its parts are seen in proportions and connections different from the truth. But this is not all. His own mind is not in the orderly and healthful state that truth demands. A portion of his understanding still slumbers within him, as truly as when all his powers were wrapped in their germ during his earliest infancy; and yet he proceeds in all his studies, as if his mental constitution were not thus incomplete. How shall such a mind not be subject to confusion and mistake, in all its inquires after truth!

But if the case be so with regard to other departments of knowledge, how much more emphatically will the same thing be true as it respects divine truth strictly so called? Here the very objects to be contemplated, as well as their relations and connections, are of such a character, that they can never be apprehended at all, except through the medium of a spiritual mind conversing with them by faith. We grow in knowledge here, just so far as we are brought to apprehend the very things themselves which we receive as truth, and no farther. Notions and speculations, however far they may be carried, fall short of the science of divine things, in the true sense of that term. We study in vain, as far as real science is concerned, except as we study with a believing and devotional habit of mind. Even our speculations without this, must be destitute of clearness and certainty, like the conclusions of men judging things around them in the dark. But if they were ever so correct, they would bring no real light into our souls. Faith is the light of the mind in religion.

The spirit of piety, then, is of the utmost importance to every one of you, as the proper life and strength of your studies. As was remarked a little while since, it cannot fail to operate favorably in this respect, by bringing the principles and motives of religion to bear upon you as students, in favor of all right habits as to the use of your time and the improvement of your privileges. But in addition to this, it will shed reality and interest on the great things with which your studies are conversant, causing them to stand out in their true, distinct, and intelligible forms, and clothing them with the splendor and magnificence of the living relations which belong to them in truth. In the very exercise of apprehending and conversing with truth in this way, the powers of the mind will be quickened and enlarged. In such circumstances the student will find in the Word of God itself all the stimulus and aliment to his studies, which are needed to make them as active and successful as they ought to be.

Cultivate piety, then, in order to gain knowledge. Let it be settled as a fixed maxim in your minds, that the spirit of prayer is the proper spirit of study. It is always a heartless and profitless business, to be employed with theological inquiries, without an inward sense of the things to which they relate, and a frame of mind congruous with the character of these things as they are in themselves.

II. But again: The cultivation of piety is of the first consequence to everyone of you, as it respects your own comfort in the trying service to which you are devoted

In any circumstances, life is a difficult burden to be borne without the animating hopes of religion. The spirit of man is not sufficient to sustain the weight of its own existence in this world, except with much inward toil and pain, when the trials and responsibilities of it are to be encountered continually in the strength of the flesh alone, without the life-giving energy of those divine principles which it is the province of religion to supply. But if this be the case with regard to human life generally, it must necessarily hold, to a more than ordinary extent, of the Christian ministry. The more directly and exclusively any sphere of employment throws us on God and holy things, as the alpha and omega of its interest, the more absolutely heartless and toilsome will it be found to our experience, if we go into it and attempt to fill it in the spirit of the world. Those who give themselves to the ministry have need to make much of the power of godliness in their own souls; for without it, they are in danger of finding themselves, even in this world, of all men most miserable. At all events, nothing is so necessary as this, in the circumstances in which they propose to spend their lives, to secure peace, and stability, and strength to their existence. Freedom, energy, constancy, courage, patience, and hope, in the work of the ministry, are all suspended on the life of God kept up actively in the soul by faith.

In these remarks, it is taken for granted that you will not take refuge from the trials of the sacred office, by hardening your hearts against its claims, and turning it into a mere form with which to cover and sanctify the wickedness of a worldly mind; or at least, that you do not now deliberately purpose any such iniquity, in seeking this solemn vocation. There is such a thing as escaping the special difficulties of the ministry in this way, by departing from God instead of drawing nigh to him and taking hold of his strength. The ministry may be secularized in the mind of its miserable incumbent, so as to be no better than the profession of a lawyer, or the trade of a politician, taken up on worldly principles and pursued for worldly ends. And although even in these circumstances it can hardly fail, by reason of its constantly recurring references to things unseen and eternal, to be attended with more discomfort to an ungodly man than avocations strictly secular, that derive their meaning and importance mainly from the present world; still it is possible that, in the midst of blunted sensibilities and slumbering consideration, he may be enabled to occupy his place from year to year with very much the same sort of self-possession and self-enjoyment, as fall to the lot of his carnal neighbors in other conditions of life. But who among us would choose an alternative so horrible as this, in order to be secured from the trials incident to the ministry, under some right sense of its awful claims? Who among us is not ready to exclaim, "Let me be chained to the very cross of my Master, rather than that I should ever be abandoned to the power of a reprobate and infidel heart, in this prostituting the glorious gospel of the grace of God to the purposes of my own selfishness."

But if our minds be not thus insensible, how shall we stand it to preach Christ and his cross continually to a stupid and gainsaying world, if he dwell not deeply in our hearts by faith and love! How shall we be instant, in season and out of season, in the work of winning souls, if the fire of divine love stir us not up to a holy passion for this glorious object! How shall we endure, year after year in carrying forward the laborious details of the ministry, through bad report as well as good report, and against the reigning tide of thought and feeling all about us, if we abide not in active fellowship with God, and heaven, and the powers of the world to come! There are, indeed, other influences that may come in, and will come in, more or less, to impart the show of animation and vigor to our public services, where these higher principles are but partially felt; but, alas, these minister no relief to the spirit that is sufficiently alive to feel its need of strictly evangelical impulses and supports, in the work of the gospel. They only make it the more painfully sensible of its own weakness and misery, in being so destitute of divine strength. To such a spirit, it is no comfort to be capable of earnestness and zeal in a religious direction, when these qualities are found, under careful analysis, resolving themselves into the spirit of party, or the thirst of praise, the pride of power, or the mere wrath of man that worketh not the righteousness of God. The tendency to our corrupt nature thus to throw itself upon the flesh rather than the spirit, even in the service of God, painfully understood and felt by the serious minister, forms of itself one of his heaviest occasions of trial. The moment he meets the world in this way, in the sphere of its own sympathies, his heart charges him with sin; and he has the witness in himself, that whatever credit he may have for zeal or power, he is not serving God in the Spirit of his Son Jesus Christ, and must fail so far, accordingly, of all real success in his ministry. Over all these difficulties, the discouragements that rise out of his own heart, and the discouragements that meet him at every step from collision with a world that has no sympathy with the objects of his peculiar vocation, the minister triumphs, if he ever triumph at all, only by entering into active communion with God, and maintaining firm hold in his spirit upon the invisible realities of faith. In this view nothing can ever be so important to him as the life of holiness in his own soul. It is this alone, which can enable him steadily to magnify his office, and to draw from it those vast and mighty motives to action, which are incorporated in its constitution beyond all that can be furnished from the whole range of life's interests besides. It is this alone, which can bring him to set his face as a flint against the friendship of the world in all its forms, and arm him at the same time with the courage of a martyr, to endure all the opposition, and indifference, and scorn, that can be heaped upon him at its hands. It is this alone, which can ever rescue him effectually from the power of the flesh in his own mind, and bring him to merge the idea of self in all its forms in Jesus Christ and him crucified, as the wisdom of God and the power of God for every purpose the ministry is designed to secure.

    As you value, then, your own peace and comfort in that life which is before you, I charge you to lay up betimes a good foundation of piety against the time to come. You know not now, as you will know hereafter, the true character of the trials you are to encounter. With all the knowledge you have acquired of yourselves, and all the observation you have taken of the world, I have no doubt that the prospect of the future is still deeply touched with the colorings of romance to your deceived vision. You may, indeed, include in your view many forms of self-denial, and labor, and trial; but on the field of your imagination even these are easily invested with a sort of sentimental charm, that strips them of all real force. It is only when we descend from those visions, to grapple with life in its unromantic details, that we come to understand what the trials of the ministry really mean. Then it is, that they begin to meet us, with thickening array, from points where we dreamed not of danger, and in forms that entered not before into our calculation; and we are brought to discover, that in being faithful to our awful commission, self-renunciation and self-denial are required to enter as very elements into our entire character, and to mingle with every part of our work. It is not to be expected, that you should fully comprehend at present in what shape you will be called upon hereafter, to deny yourselves and take up the cross and follow Christ; but of this be sure, that many trials and afflictions abide you, and that the very highest wisdom of which you are capable as candidates for the sacred office, is to arm yourselves for them with the power of godliness.

It is a reflection also which you should lay to heart, that the times on which you are fallen are likely to try you with unusual severity. There are periods in the church, when the stream of things flows with so smooth and evenly a course, that Christians and Christian ministers are, to a certain extent, borne up and carried along in their place, independently of their own exertions. But such is not the period on which the church in this country is now entering. The foundations of thought have begun in some measure to give way. Action and reaction are powerfully at work in the whole system of mind. Principles are coming to be unsettled. Passion and the spirit of party are blending themselves with all moral inquiries and all practical interests. The wrath of man, that delights itself in the earthquake, whirlwind, and fire, is pushing itself fearfully forward in the place of the still small voice of Heaven. And is there no special call upon you, my young friends, in these circumstances, to prepare yourselves for the mighty conflict that is before you, by taking earnest hold upon God? Alas! what will your strength avail, in the midst of these storms and billows of temptation, if the power of a divine life be not deeply wrought into your very being! Assuredly, without this, you will make shipwreck of your ministry, as far as its true ends are concerned. You will lose sight of the truth, and forsake it for the bewildering phantoms of worldly reason. You will sacrifice to pride, and self-will, and noise, the fruits of the Spirit, and the power of the Spirit, as comprehended only in the meek and lowly patience of Jesus Christ. You will be driven by a legion of demons into the wilderness and among the tombs; or engulfed, sooner or later, in the overwhelming sweep of those dark waters, over which the spirit of party broods in perpetual tumult and storm.

III. Again, you are bound to cultivate piety in order that you may be useful

Piety is not indeed the only qualification that is needed to make you successful in the ministry; but it ought never to be forgotten, that it is the great qualification for this purpose, and of more consequence than all you can possess besides. No amount of advantages without it, can make up for its absence. In your circumstances emphatically it is true, that religion is the principal thing, and that all things you can desire besides are not to be compared with it for value. Though I speak with the tongues of men and angels, without this I am no better than sounding brass. Though I have all knowledge and all power to sustain me, as a teacher of righteousness, if this be wanting it profiteth me nothing.

    No idea can be more unreasonable, than to suppose that the ends of the Christian ministry may be answered to any extent, without an inward correspondence in him who exercises the solemn trust with its own sacred and heavenly character. "The words that I speak unto you," Jesus Christ has said, "they are *spirit and life."* And how then can they be faithfully represented by a spiritual automation, wrought upon and moved by the dead mechanism only of human instruction! It is only as the gospel is made to live in the soul, and utter its sound from the midst of living affections, that it becomes properly intelligible, or is made to arrest the attention of the world with its proper power. In this sense only the disciples of Christ are constituted his witnesses, and in this sense only can the ministry be considered as the real "testimony of Jesus." We preach in vain, if we cannot say, "I believe and therefore speak." Occasional instances may occur of salutary impression from the ministrations of a carnal minister, or as it has sometimes been expressed, the bones of a dead prophet *may* be employed to raise a corpse to life; but such cases are out of the common order of things, and in a measure unnatural. To make the gospel felt, as a general thing, we must feel it ourselves. There is a deeper language necessary than that of words, to reach and move the foundations of character. The love of God must be in us, and the faith of Christ, and a true inward concern for the souls of our fellow men, before we can influence them much in favor of the claims of religion. These sentiments, where they exist, convey themselves from mind to mind by a sort of deep sympathetic communication, breathing through the ordinary outward forms of expression in a way not easily described but universally felt, which no art can ever effectually imitate; and they open the doors of the heart, for the introduction of truth, where argument alone and eloquence might have been employed for ever without effect. This is the true secret of a pious minister's strength. He speaks with authority, because conviction and compassion accompany all his words. *His* simple testimony is of more weight than the reasonings of other men, however learned and profound. The very sight of him is adapted to make a good impression; for he carries about with him the credentials of a holy man of God; and when he opens his mouth for Christ, he seems to say with something of the sublime confidence of John, *"That which was from the beginning, which we have heard, which we have seen with our eyes, which we have looked upon, and our hands have handled of the word of life; that which we have seen and heard, declare we unto you, that ye also may have fellowship with us; and truly our fellowship is with the Father and with his Son, Jesus Christ."*

Let it sink deeply into your hearts, that the very highest and by far the most acceptable contribution of service you can render to God and his cause in the world, is comprehended in the light and power of holiness embodied and made real in your own lives. On this our Lord Jesus Christ relied pre-eminently, in the case of his own ministry, to the exclusion of all those forms of power with which men commonly are accustomed to seek the accomplishment of their purposes. This constituted the greatness and strength of the apostles; won its mighty triumphs for the Christianity of primitive times; and wrought the wonders of the Reformation, in the days of Luther and the men who hazarded their lives with him for the truth. And this it is, which more than all resources besides, the church now needs for the successful prosecution of her proper work; since God has ordained this to be her strength, and all hope of converting the world without it is idle in the extreme. The outward machinery of her benevolence may extend; and facilities and opportunities for doing good be multiplied indefinitely; and the treasury of the Lord be made to overflow with silver and gold, and the favor of the high and mighty be enlisted in support of every Christian enterprise; and the strong, heavy force of public opinion, organized and concentrated by voluntary associations, be turned with effect against every high thing that exalteth itself visible against truth and righteousness; and yet all will prove valueless in the end for the true kingdom of Christ, if the action of holiness be not found in the church itself. Other things that promise well to the eye of man are at best but auxiliary to the power of the gospel, and in many cases they stand at war with it altogether, by thrusting themselves into its place. But the holiness of the church, is the power of the gospel itself, which is to secure for it the victory of the world. Your ministry, then, will be profitable to the world and honorable to God, exactly to the extent in which it shall be found to contribute to this interest. And this character it will have just according to the measure of your own piety, and no farther. Beyond this, you will have no disposition, or knowledge, or power to proceed, in laboring for the piety of others.

Be persuaded, then, to cultivate holiness that you may live to the greatest purpose in your coming ministry. Resolve to bring unto God, in this service, the power of a holy mind, which is of great price in his sight. If such be your honest resolution, you need not fear that you shall live in vain, or to little purpose. God himself will see to it, that your ministry shall not be lost to the world. It will be worth immeasurably more to the world, than millions of money in your hands to use for religion, or all the interest and policy of the world doing homage to the same cause at your feet. It will place you in a better position for usefulness, than the widest field of notoriety that birth, or station, or popular accomplishments can ever open to the influence of a single man. You may live in a single narrow corner of the earth, and yet God can cause your influence to reach nations and continents, that have never heard of your name. You may wear out your days in obscurity, and die without renown, and yet God can raise your name from the dust, and send it down, as a part of his own glorious testimony for the truth, to all coming generations. You may drop into the grave at the very threshold of your work, and yet God can fix your memory, like that of James Brainerd Taylor, as a star in the firmament of righteousness above men's heads, that shall light more souls to glory when you are dead, than the ministry of a hundred years could have done, under ordinary circumstances, in the world.

IV. Once more: you owe it to yourselves to cultivate personal religion in order that you may make your own calling and election sure

You will not be surprised, that I should press you with this consideration, as well as the others that have been mentioned. It is a common fancy in the church that ministers are, by their profes-

Lecture Three

sion, to a great extent secure from the dangers that beset the way to heaven, as it must be traveled by other men. But it may be presumed, that no such thought is harbored in your minds. You know that sacred studies and sacred employments are no safeguard, of themselves, to inward godliness. The horns of the altar, in this sense, offer no protection from danger. Ministers and candidates for the ministry, as others, have need to be exhorted and stirred up to watchfulness continually, lest their hearts be hardened through the deceitfulness of sin, and they come short of the glory of God in the end.

All this is fully implied in the strong terms used with regard to the circumstances of ministers in the New Testament. Some of the most solemn admonitions of Jesus Christ, with regard to the danger of being found unfaithful and unsound at the last, were addressed to those very disciples whom he had selected to be Apostles in the work of the gospel. And accordingly we hear no less a man than Paul, in the midst of his labors afterwards exclaiming, "I so run, not as uncertainly; so fight I, not as one that beateth the air: but I keep under my body and bring it into subjection; lest that by any means, when I have preached to others, I myself should be cast-away."

The whole ministry of the church, from the beginning, abounds with awful instruction on the same subject. The ministry has been very far from being a sanctuary of righteousness and salvation, to the great body of those, who, in different ages of the church, have adventured upon its holy functions. It has been a savor of death unto death, instead of a savor of life unto life, unto thousands and tens of thousands, that have borne its honors and responsibilities before the world. More ministers have been lost, than have ever been saved. Hell has more of them to boast of than heaven.

Indeed it is only necessary to consider the circumstances of temptation with which the sacred office is surrounded in the world, in connection with the known character of the human heart, to be convinced that it is an exceedingly perilous position for any but the most vigilant to occupy. The deceitfulness of the heart is not destroyed, nor in the least degree impaired, by an outward consecration to theological studies; while, at the same time, the forms and relations that are thus assumed, are in the highest degree adapted to encourage and aid the treacherous workings to which it is always inclined. It is one of the easiest things in the world, and one of the most common in the church, to mistake official sacredness for personal religion; and fearfully manifold are the ways, in which the man, whose lips and hands are familiar with holy things, and who is accustomed to challenge for himself the credit of a scribe in all that pertains to religion, and whose piety, if it be only authenticated with the common decencies of his profession, no man feels himself at liberty to question, while most have an interest rather in taking the genuineness of it for granted on the lowest score of pretension, as the easy standard of duty for themselves—fearfully manifold, I say, are the ways in which such a man may escape the strong power of truth, and make his place a cloak for his sins to hide them even from the eye of his own conscience, and flatter himself in his own sight, till his iniquity shall become hateful only in the light of the judgment day.

Resolve, then, now, in the strength of God's grace, to save your own souls from the shipwreck of the second death. It should terrify you certainly to think of being damned, with the title of *Reverend* upon your head. It were better to descend to hell from any other height, than that you should go down thither from the sacred desk. Let your resolution be taken, then, now, within the walls of this seminary, to make your calling and election sure. Consider it part of your necessary preparation for that perilous office to which you are looking, to have your souls so strengthened in the principles of piety, that when you shall hereafter be thrown forth upon the world, there may be no danger of your falling away from your own steadfastness. You will never have a more favorable time, than at present, for attending to this great interest. And it ought to be distinctly considered by every one of you, that whether you mean it to be so or not, the spirit you carry with you through seminary will determine, most prob-

Lecture Three

ably, so far as religion is concerned, the complexion of all your future character. The character of the minister may in some instances prove highly spiritual (the result of God's powerful discipline after entrance on its active duties), where the character of the student has been of another sort; but this is not the ordinary and natural order of things, and it can be no better than wicked presumption for any to comfort themselves, in your situation, with the hope of becoming hereafter in this respect what you are not striving to be now. Those who have had any opportunity of observing, know that the spirit which candidates for the ministry have in the theological seminary, is almost universally the spirit which they carry along with them as ministers into the church, and that continues to distinguish them through life. The conscientious student makes the conscientious pastor. The serious, prayerful, heavenly-minded candidate, is known afterwards as the good shepherd of souls, who walks in the steps of Jesus Christ, and lays himself out in labors of love for the salvation of men. While, on the other hand, show me a careless, idle, self-indulgent student, and I behold one whose ministry also will be characterized by carelessness and sloth. Show me a proud, passionate, self-willed student, and I see in him one that will preach himself hereafter more than Christ, and spread difficulty and trouble around him in the church. Show me a theological dandy, under the name and garb of a candidate for the ministry, who affects to incorporate the spirit of fashion with religion, in order that he may recommend it the better to the world; who is always pleading for gentility and declaiming against monkishness, as an apology for the lightness and worldliness of his own carriage; who spends as much time at his toilet, as he does upon his knees in secret prayer; whose books are abandoned, and his room vacated, on every call to enter into company; who delights in mixed society, where he can be allowed to *unbend* himself from the fatigues of study, in unrestrained sympathy with the frivolous spirit of the youthful and gay around him, with only a sentimental reflection, that sounds like religion, brought in from time to time to sanctify the occasion; who by smooth gallantries wins for himself, in spite of all the disadvantages of his station, and deserves to wear, the laurels of a "ladies man"; show me such a *theological dandy*, in pumps and gloves, and I need no prophet's inspiration to foretell, that he will be neither a son of thunder nor of consolation to the church, in time to come. His name will not be great in Israel; and more are likely to fall than shall ever rise, under the curse of his ministry.

Here, then, I say again, in the theological seminary, you owe it to your own souls to look well to your personal piety. Try yourselves diligently whether you be in the faith. Do not easily take it for granted that you are safe in this respect. And at the same time be always pressing onwards in the way to perfection. Take firm hold of the everlasting covenant. Prove what is the good, and acceptable and perfect will of God in Jesus Christ. Give all diligence to understand the gospel, as ordained of God for the sanctification of believers; and to have your entire character brought under the control of strictly evangelical motives, in distinction from such as belong only to this world. Aim, in one of the favorite expressions of that sainted youth, whose named has been already mentioned, to be "uncommon Christians." This will require you to come out from the world, to be separate from its maxims and fashions, to set the Lord always before you, to yield yourselves up honestly to the idea of Christian discipleship, in denying yourselves, forsaking all, and following the blessed Redeemer. But it will bring with it its own exceeding great reward. There is no other way in which you can do so much for yourselves, or for the church, or for the world. In thus following the Lord fully, you may expect your peace to flow as a river, in the midst of all outward discouragements, down to the end of life. Your strength will rise continually with your age, so that you shall mount up with wings as eagles, and run and not be weary, in the service of God. Though your outward man fail, your inward man shall be renewed day by day. In the midst of all distractions and commotions, all strong trials and floods of temptation, you will be enabled to possess your souls in the calm independence of truth, and to endure unto the end as seeing

Lecture Three

Him who is invisible. Holiness is power, in the very highest sense of the expression. Other forms of strength are poor in comparison with it, for all purposes, whether of influence on others or of defense and support for yourselves. And no other is so entirely within the scope of your faculties and opportunities. It is only a few that can expect to make much impression on the world, by their learning and eloquence, or the daring originality of their views. But there is not one of you, who may not calculate certainly on being able to wield a far more important influence in the ministry, if he does but honestly resolve to excel in "the same mind that was in Christ Jesus." All of you have it in your power thus, to become burning and shining lights in your generation. By surrendering yourselves to this object, as your great ruling interest, you cannot fail to have authority and to do good in the church. You will not live in vain. God will clothe you with honor even in this world, in the midst of all tribulations through which your work may require you to pass. And to crown all, having turned many to righteousness, you shall shine as the brightness of the firmament, in heaven, and as the stars for ever and ever.

Lecture Four
Evangelical Motives

Whom I serve with my Spirit, in the Gospel of his Son. (Romans 1:9)

In religion, all may be said to turn upon the state of the mind, as determined by its affections and principles of action, rather than by its mere knowledge and intellectual operations.

"God is a spirit, and they that worship him must worship him in Spirit and in truth." Outward services may be required as the proper expression of such worship, but it is only when actuated with the living sense of devotion that they can have any value in his sight. And the most lofty contemplations of genius, as well as the most profound and comprehensive research of science, even when employed with holy things, are just as little sufficient of themselves to constitute the true idea of piety. Bodily forms and forms of the understanding are alike hollow and vain, except as far as they may enshrine the power of a divine life within, and show themselves to be instructed with the Spirit of it continually.

What is thus true of religion in general, cannot fail of course to hold good in the work of the Christian ministry in particular. It is a trust that cannot be discharged by any outward activities merely, however laborious and manifold, and however suitable in themselves to the end which it is proposed to reach. Nor will any resources of thought or eloquence be sufficient to meet its claims, however vigorously exercised for the purpose. There is needed over and above this all, a certain position of the soul relative to the great truths of religion, in the sentiments and affections which make up its secret life. The right state of the soul in this respect, forms the great fundamental requisition for the sacred office. It is that to which God mainly looks in calling men to this trust, and without which none are called of him, however excellently fitted they may seem to be by other advantages for the work. Whatever men themselves may think, he makes no account at all of zeal, or eloquence or learning, unsanctified by a divine life within for the purpose he aims to accomplish by the ministry. And we may be sure, that his judgment in this case, as in every other, is in accordance with truth. The proper idea of the ministry, includes this view of its character. This right state of mind enters essentially into the definition of this work. Where it is wanting, we may have indeed much that is imposing and stirring in the outward man; and the world may even be filled with admiration of splendid endowments and ample resources, which are thus made tributary as it would seem to the service of the sanctuary. But after all, the service will be only as a dead carcass, fair to look upon, and full of promise to the eye, but the semblance only of what it claims to be, and insufficient altogether, for the purposes of life which the ministry is designed to reach. The soul of the ministry is found in the view and motives, answerable to the high intention, which reign within the true Ambassador of Heaven, and urge him to spend and be spent in his work. Other advantages may be important as auxiliary to the character in which he appears among men, but this is a qualification which reaches to the very foundation of the whole trust and belongs indispensable to the truth of his character itself. This it is alone, which can properly sustain a man in the duties of the ministry, or clothe him with the proper power of his office.

It is always, then, of the first movement of those who are already in office, and to those who aspire to it, as students of theology, not only to try themselves frequently with regard to the actual state of their souls in the view now considered; but to study and labor systematically also for the improvement of their own character in this respect. This right state of mind, relative to divine things, which we have seen, constitutes the life and power of the sacred ministry, is not to be secured to any extent or maintained for any time, without much attention and diligence on our part, directed to this end. It is not enough, that we may have been brought to have some sense of the power of spiritual motives. We need to be subdued to their influence continually more and more, until our whole character may be changed into a corresponding complexion, and other principles of action swallowed up in their constant strength. But this can take place only by means of a steady diligence on our part, contemplating specifically this end. The work of sanctification, in general, is advanced in this way. The mind must be turned earnestly to the cultivation of the different forms of character which make up the idea of holiness, laboring to be invested with them in detail, before any progress will be made in this blessed business. And so in the case now before us, the spirit of the ministry, which to us indeed may be said to comprehend a large part of our sanctification itself, must be cultivated seriously and perseveringly by a proper attention to the particular forms of mind in which it may be said to consist, connected with all suitable endeavors to make them fully our own. And what I wish particularly to press here upon your consideration, is the duty of regarding this, in all your preparatory training for the sacred office, as the most necessary part of the whole. It will be a melancholy mistake, indeed with any of you, if, in the midst of other studies and exercises, designed to make you hereafter workmen that "need not be ashamed," this fundamental interest, the spirit of the work itself, should be overlooked and left to the care of itself. Be assured, no diligence you can bestow on other pursuits, and no

Lecture Four

success with which it is possible for them to be crowned, will ever compensate for negligence or unfaithfulness here. If you are wise, you will not think of waiting till you go into the work itself, for the sentiments and feelings which are needed to carry you through it with comfort and success. You will look upon this as the "one thing needful" in your undertaking, and your hearts will be set upon it now. And it is not too much to say of any theological student, who allows himself to forget this interest, or makes but small account of it, that he is unfaithful to his vocation, and false to his assumed character. The man is not fit to prepare for the ministry certainly, who thinks the spirit of the office may safely be expected to rise within hereafter from the occasions of the office itself; or who holds it to be enough for this purpose to cultivate as he may think a religious character in general, without descending to particular endeavors turned this way, as a part of his regular and proper education.

With the view of assisting you in the prosecution of this great work, as well as to stir you up to a serious consideration of its claims, I propose now to call your attention to some leading forms of feeling, in which I suppose the spirit of the ministry mainly consists. They may be denominated *evangelical motives* as distinguished from all inferior principles by which it is possible for men to be governed in the sacred office, where these are wanting. And before proceeding to consider them directly, it may be well to refer cursorily to some of the spurious principles which are thus substituted too often for the true spirit of the work. We need to be put frequently on our guard against these, as well as, to be stirred up to the cultivation of a higher order of character; though the only way, indeed, in which we can effectually purge ourselves of their presence, is to fetch into them, by the grace of God, the views and feelings which make up the higher order of character itself. By our entering into the sense of evangelical motives, we escape the power of those which are earthly; by learning to walk in the Spirit, we cease to fulfill the lusts of the flesh.

A man may enter into the sacred office, with the view of providing comfortably for his own wants in the present world. Or if he should not be conscious at all of any such view when he enters the ministry, it may turn out to his experience the most operative stimulus to him in his work afterwards. In this way the ministry is degraded to the level of ordinary occupations of life. And when this feeling has come to prevail, it will not stop in a simple care for necessary wants, such as food and raiment, but will run out in the form of active covetousness, the common idolatry of the world in its other pursuits. There is great danger, more than in your present circumstances you can well understand, of your succumbing hereafter to this low and base affection so as to make the altar of God itself tributary to its power.

Again, the credit which belongs to the condition of a clergyman, and the refined and honorable ease which is supposed to go along with his profession, may be a reason for seeking the office; and the same general feeling may operate afterwards to carry men regularly forward in the discharge of many of its outward duties. This sentiment is closely allied to the first one mentioned; though in some cases, it may make a much more elaborate character by linking itself with a literary taste.

Again, the desire of distinction may be the reigning motive, in embracing the sacred profession and performing afterwards the services it requires. With some the general credit of the profession itself is not enough, they must make it to themselves the path way to honor and power. They are carried away with the desire of being seen and known of men. They affect eminence of some sort, in their own sphere. They may labor in this way to secure reputation of learning. Or they may aspire to the praise of great eloquence in the pulpit, or they may set their hearts upon making a conspicuous figure in the politics of the church. Or they may propose even to shine, as patterns of zeal and diligence in laboring to stem the torrent of sin which is in the world, and turn men to righteousness. To name such motives is at once to expose them to the reprobation of all serious persons. But alas! What a task it is to expel the principle of them from the soul. It is a great thing to be made superior to these low springs of action, so as to be able to study, and cultivate every gift, and use every resource, and labor in public as well as in private, truly and simply for God without seeking to exalt ourselves. And yet just so far as we fall short of this victory, deriving our stimulus and support in action from the presence of the world and not from the presence of God, we shall be wanting in both skill and strength for every part of our work.

Once more; the simple sense of duty connected as it must be with the strong persuasion of the wickedness of man, and the claims of the gospel, may work powerfully upon a man in the ministry and yet leave him comparatively without strength. He may have a serious impression of the sacredness of his work and of the responsibilities which it involves, such as will make it impossible for him to be satisfied with a mere mechanical round of services of any kind. He may have his mind set on spiritual results in his ministry, and feel strongly the untractable material with which he is called to work in the character of the world; and he may then identify himself with the cause of religion, in such a way as to be very earnest oftentimes in pleading it against the spirit by which it is opposed. But all this may belong to his experience without any clear and steady hold in his own mind on the great evangelical views from which the true and proper power of the ministry proceeds; and then it will be in his own spirit, and according to the flesh, after all, that every effort will proceed which he may be engaged to make. His zeal will mix itself continually with the bitterness of human passion. His resolution for God will always be merging itself in the violence of self-will. He will continually fall into sin while endeavoring to correct sin in others, and thus find himself inwardly shorn of strength, at the very moment when he may have the greatest show of it outwardly.

I propose now to notice those principles of action in which I suppose the spirit of the ministry properly to consist, and which are adequate to sustain and animate the soul in the midst of its heavy responsibilities. It is by fixing your attention on these and then laboring to have them wrought into the structure of your interior life, that you may hope to clean yourselves from all filthiness of the spirit, such as we have just been contemplating, and to offer your lives to God, in this service as living sacrifices, holy and acceptable through Jesus Christ.

I. I mention first, the sense of a divine commission

The ministry is God's work; and those who are rightly in the office, are in it by special election and investiture from Heaven. They are not only called to it by the Providence of God, but have been solemnly set apart by it also, like Paul and Barnabas of old, by the Holy Ghost. "We are Ambassadors for Christ," says the Apostle, "as though God did beseech you by us, we pray you in Christ's stead, be ye reconciled to God." So to the elders at Ephesus, "Take heed unto yourselves, to all the flock over which the Holy Ghost has made you overseers." And it is always supposed in the case, that those who are thus distinguished should bear about with them habitually in their work a solemn sense, and recollection of the character which belongs to them in this respect. They are required to attend upon the duties of the sacred office, as fulfilling them until the Lord. Now it is an easy thing for men to take hold of this idea in a fleshly way, arrogating to themselves the credit and authority of such a commission, on the ground of their official standing in the visible church, or from the imagination only which they have of being divinely called into the ministry; so as to the lord it at times, over God's heritage, and to utter great swelling words of vanity, making themselves more prominent than Him whose cause they affect to represent. But it is something vastly more difficult to bring the mind into a dire, sober, and steady sense of ministerial character, as involving this relation to God, and the invisible world without any sort of exaggeration or figure. This is a feeling which cannot have place except where the idea it embraces is a reality. Mere fancy cannot form the soul to it, under any circumstances. It can result only from faith, apprehending spiritual relations as they are, and conveying the power of them into the living sense of the mind where it reigns. Difficult, however, as it is to reach and hold this elevated position, there can be no freedom nor strength in the work of the ministry from any other point of action. Rightly apprehended the sense of a divine commission has no tendency whatever to lift a man up with pride; its tendency is all in an opposite direction; but it is needed to inspire him with a just confidence in the claims of his office, and a proper courage in the discharge of his duties. It is only the man who feels that he is acting from God and for God, in the ministry, that can be expected to speak, and act with becoming liberty, firmness and energy, in the performance of his work. Thus we find the Apostle Paul frequently referring to this consideration, as one that served in the highest degree to animate and nerve him for the service to which he was called. "I thank Christ Jesus our Lord, who hath enabled me, for that he counted me faithful, putting me into the ministry." "Unto me who am less than the least of all the saints, is this grace given, that I should preach among the Gentiles, the unsearchable riches of Christ." "Though I preach the Gospel I have nothing to glory of; for necessity is laid upon me; yea, woe is me, if I preach not the Gospel; for if I do this thing willingly, I have a reward; but if against my will, a dispensation of the Gospel committed unto me."

II. *A proper sense of the dignity of the work itself*

"I magnify mine office," says Paul, and every minister should be able to do the same thing. This he cannot fail to do to a certain extent if he has within him that persuasion of acting under divine commission, of which I have first spoken. That must necessarily be considered a great and honorable work which a man is called to perform by a direct and special appointment from God himself. But the feeling of which I now speak reaches beyond this idea so as to include some just estimate of the intrinsic excellence and glory of the work itself. Here again, it is easy for the flesh, under certain circumstances, to counterfeit the judgment of the Spirit and to put honor on the sacred office for things that may be adventitiously connected with it, without any perception at all of its true spiritual dignity. But the minister who magnifies his office truly does it always on grounds which the world can neither understand nor approve. The naked ministry of reconciliation having for its object the restoration of sinners to the image and favor of God, which to the carnal eye is an interest as much without form or comeliness as the person of the Redeemer himself, is that which is looked upon in this case as the loftiest and most brilliant service to which a man can consecrate his life. No matter under what circumstances of external meanness and obscurity it may be prosecuted, it is felt to carry with it, wrapped up in its own divine constitution, a glory that throws into the shade the splendor of the highest official distinctions that are known besides among men. To see this, as something more than a dream or fancy, or a dogma of the understanding requires faith. In every proper estimate of the ministry, there is involved the power of substantiating spiritual ideas and asserting the high and eternal superiority of all that is moral to all that is comprehended only in the world of sense. Here dwells the inherent grandeur of the office. It is an embassy from heaven. It occupies itself with the interests of the soul. Its transaction takes hold every moment upon the invisible world, and looks far forward in to the depths of eternity. And it is the sense of all this that is wanted to form the minister to an inward frame corresponding to his high vocation. Nothing less will avail to sustain him and carry him forward in his work. Without this, he will always be in danger of despising his office, and certainly can never glory in it, and give himself wholly to it, as he should. But where this right judgment prevails, the ministry will be found to be its own exceeding great reward. What, suppose you, could have persuaded Paul to exchange his vocation for any other service the world had to offer him? His soul was captivated with the idea of the ministry itself; and it was not in the power of poverty and disgrace, or stripes and chains, to put him out of love with it, or to make him think for one moment of discharging himself from its claims.

III. A due apprehension of the presence and glory of God, connected with the desire of pleasing him and a lively fear of not finding acceptance in his presence at last

Where any proper views are entertained of the nature of the sacred office itself, they cannot fail to carry along with them some measure also of this feeling. If a man looks upon himself as acting under a divine commission, his eye will be turned toward the author of that commission, and he will feel the necessity of commending himself in every part of his work to the judgment of God, rather than to the opinions of men. And so far as the mind has become enlightened to discern and approve the glory of the office, it must delight also in the character of God, and be supremely solicitous to secure and enjoy his favor. It is easy to see, however, how important and necessary this inward habit is for the man who is called to preach the Gospel, and how diligently it ought to be cultivated by all who aspire to this work. This forms the true minister's strength, in opposition to all human authority arrayed against him. This places him above the frowns and smiles of the world alike. This makes his eye single, and his heart true to the proper end of his office. "With me," says Paul, "it is a very small thing that I should be judged by you, or of man's judgment; yea, I judge not mine own self, for I know nothing of myself, yet am I not hereby justified: but he that judgeth me is the Lord." "We are not as many which corrupt the Word of God; but as of sincerity, but as of God, in the sight of God, speak we in Christ." "Knowing the terror of the Lord, we persuade men, but are made manifest unto God." "I so run, not as uncertainty; so fight I not as one that beateth the air, but I keep under my body and bring it into subjection; lest that by any means, when I have preached to others, I myself should be cast away."

IV. Active love for the souls of men

The great end of the ministry is the salvation of souls. The son of man came into the world to seek and save the lost. And this object he continues to prosecute from age to age, by the agency particularly of those whom he commissions to preach the Gospel. "I will make you," says he, "fishers of men." The commission is, "Go ye into all the world and preach the gospel to every creature." "He that believeth and is baptized shall be saved, but he that believeth not shall be damned." The spirit of the work then is lodged here. It cannot be understood or felt, without a lively apprehension of the worth of the soul, and an active desire to save men from sin and hell. Other objects which the ministry may be made to contemplate, however important, will not be found sufficient to take the place of this great central end. The business of those who are in it is to "watch for souls, as those who must give account," but if they have not sense of the greatness of this interest in its own nature, so as to derive animation and strength from it for their work, how can they be expected to proceed in it as they should? Their ministry without this cannot fail to be mechanical and artificial. The spring will be wanting that should set it in action. But this love of souls is not in any of us naturally. Sin makes us selfish and indifferent to the welfare of others; and it exalts the flesh besides above all that belongs to the Spirit; so that even where natural affection may engage us to seek the happiness of those we love, we are prone to expend our interest wholly on their physical and temporal wants to the utter exclusion of those which the Gospel is designed to reach. We require a new nature, then, in order that we not only truly desire the happiness of others, but make more account also of their spiritual interests for this end, than of all other considerations. And this divine sentiment we are to cultivate with the utmost pains, that all selfish feelings and carnal views may be subdued continually more and more to its power; as it is only in this way that we can enter into the reason, or understand the Spirit, or be clothed with the strength of the office to which we are called. The man who does not take pains to form himself to the Spirit which was in Jesus Christ in this respect, is not fit to enter the ministry and cannot be expected to occupy it with comfort to himself or benefit to others.

V. A proper confidence in the doctrine of the cross, as the only help for a ruined world

It is not enough that we have a deep sense of the wretched circumstances, in which mankind are as sinners, or that we be actuated by a strong desire of extending to them the relief they need; we must be able also to appreciate aright the power and sufficiency of the remedy which the gospel itself has provided for this end. This, however, is something above mere nature. The doctrine of the cross is foolishness to the carnal mind, and seems to have no suitableness whatever for the object it is proposed to reach by its means. It requires a spiritual education to discern the true glory of it in this respect, so as to be able to rely upon it fully and steadily in laboring for the welfare of the world. The difficulty is not indeed to retain the notion of the doctrine, and to make great account of it in word. This may be done through the presence merely of the general state of opinion around us. But nothing is more common than to be ignorant of the true glory of the cross under the semblance of great respect for it, as the cardinal idea of the gospel; and oftentimes the name and notion are employed to disguise from other forms of thought altogether, and this so effectually that the error is not perceived even by those who are the subjects of it; it may be during their whole life. To see the real glory of the cross and to understand the power of it for all the great purposes of the gospel salvation, and the relation in which it stands to gospel holiness, as well as to the pardon of sin, is a faculty which few possess. And yet nothing is more imperiously demanded for the work of the ministry. "I determined to know nothing among you," says Paul, "but Christ and him crucified." And again, "God forbid & c."[1] "The Jews require a sign & c."

---

[1] & c. = etc.

VI. Strong attachment to the Savior, identifying us in spirit with his life, and inspiring us with an ambition to be like him in all respects

Jesus Christ is exhibited to us in the Gospel, not merely as the great sacrifice for our sins, but as the great exemplification also to our eyes of that spiritual dignity and glory to which we are called to aspire as his followers. He is the perfect idea of holiness, reduced to a living and tangible form, in our own nature, and it is only as our souls are brought to discern the glory of his person in this respect, and to fix upon him as their great interest, that they can be delivered from the power of the world, and the dominion of those miserable lusts to which they are naturally enslaved. The strength of the gospel for all the purposes of righteousness, may be said to be comprehended in its power to imbue the soul with such an attachment to the person of the loving God, thus revealed, as it sufficient to draw it away from all opposing and conflicting interests. Our salvation is not wrought out by any process of abstract contemplation on the claims of virtue; neither is it secured by a sentiment of cold respect merely for the character of the Savior. The germ of the new life, into which it calls us, is *love*, fixing itself upon the person of Christ and powerfully working all things into our complexions. And the design of the Gospel is that this love should be of the highest and most active order, such as may identify the life of the soul with the glorious object it contemplates, and cause it to find, as it were, a new existence in the sense of an overwhelming sympathy with all that belongs to this living and satisfying interest. But if this state of mind be thus necessary to the purposes of the Gospel, in the case of all ordinary Christian experience, I need not say how indispensable it must be for the work of the ministry in particular. Here the love of the soul for Jesus Christ should take upon it the form of a passion. It should be so strong as to make the idea of his person always the great moving stimulus to action in our souls, making it our highest ambition always to be like him, in the spirit even of his suffering and death, and turning the fairest visions of life into a sterile waste for our hearts when dissociated from the fellowship of his pure and glorious mind. So felt Paul, "The love of Christ," says he "constraineth us." "I count all things but loss & c." "I fill up that which is behind & c."

VII. *The ambition of distinction in heaven*

We are to be saved, if saved at all, on the grounds exclusively of the merits of Jesus Christ, without any respect whatsoever to our own works. But it is very clearly taught in the New Testament at the same time, that our diligence and activity in the service of God will be honored with a particular regard in heaven, suitable to the nature of the case. Our salvation must be all of grace, but in full consistency with this, it will be attended with more or less glory, according to the measure of our piety in this world. Of course, there are degrees in the state of the blessed on high. And as it is fit that we should be engaged to Christian activity on the motive simply of making our own calling and election sure, so it is fit that we should have respect to this recompense of reward also, which is proposed to our faith, in the prospect of the different degrees that belong to the blessedness of the righteous in heaven. It is a mistake, which some entertain, that a notion of this kind should not be invested upon in exhorting men to religion; and it is an argument of defective spiritual sense, when Christians feel themselves but little moved by the consideration of it, in favor of the holy life. That is a poor and shriveled religion which satisfies itself with the idea of merely getting to heaven, and makes no account of the glories that lie beyond.

What is the highest distinction known in this life, the most important interest of time, in comparison with the relative worth only of one degree of glory above another, in the heavenly world? So far as we are spiritual, this consideration cannot fail to be felt.

Accordingly, it is presented in the Scriptures expressly for this purpose. Jesus Christ himself we are told was animated in all his mediatorial work by looking forward to the reward with which it was to be crowned in the end. "For the joy that was set before him, & c." So Paul, "This one thing I do & c." Ministers need to be fully alive to this animating hope in every part of their work. It is a sentiment which they should cultivate in their souls with the greatest diligence and care. General expectations of heaven are not enough. There should be a reality, a vividness, a nearness, and an overwhelming force in their hope, sufficient to carry them high above all discouragements and trials. This can be the case only where an intimate correspondence is kept up in the soul with great objects of faith, from day to day. The crown which is to be received hereafter from the Chief Shepherd, "a crown of glory that fadeth not away," must stand out to the mind as a palpable interest, outweighing, in its habitual sense, all the sacrifices by which it is to be secured. When this is the case, there will be strength such as the great ends of the ministry require.

Lecture Five

Fields of Labor

After the question of his call, the candidate must ask: What is my proper field? This is just as important as the first. The particular field will also need a divine appointment. Paul speaks of different departments filled by different persons. So it is necessary to find the particular spheres for which we are qualified. No man can enter upon the work honestly, without seeking to know the will of God in this respect. The field is the world and the question, then first would be, whether a foreign or domestic field should be chosen. These are different departments of the one and same work, and we cannot make so broad a distinction between them as is generally done, as if they were of two different orders altogether. The pastor is as acceptable as the missionary, if he labors where he is appointed to labor. Their work is equally acceptable to the Lord. This should be diligently inquired into by each one for himself, taking into view his talents, relations, God's Providence, & c. Here we can make only general remarks.

All are not called to go abroad. Some are needed, and may do more good at home. Others may do some good at home, and are not fit to go abroad. Persons of weak constitution, timid, invalid men, of mental imbecility, deficient in resources and practical tact, apt to despond, should not go abroad. Sometimes such a defect of spirit may be worse than defect of body. A sick man may have great resources and practical tact, and his disease may even be cured by going abroad. Whilst a man of mental imbecility may bring himself, and the whole mission into danger and difficulties.

In general there is not much tendency to carry the going abroad to an extreme. Such cases have however taken place. Thus under the pressure of appeal men have been forced to enter the foreign field. Thus the Crusaders under strong appeals forsook their homes and left them to perish, and went to Palestine. There was a good deal of missionary feeling and zeal shown here and it serves to show how imagination and the presence of appeals may carry hundreds into a field for which they are not qualified.

A missionary should have, after eminent piety, a good constitution, firmness, patience, readiness of resources, promptness, decisiveness. (Thus Dr. King, at Athens.) Also aptness to acquire foreign languages. We cannot measure this by tact in acquiring dead languages. It is much easier to learn a living language.

The question has been raised: Should missionaries marry? This is connected with the question whether missionaries ought to marry. The objections to this are spacious. The expenses are greater. There will not be the same devoted, self denying spirit - the wife may get sick, and this may bring the missionary from the field. Thus Catholics reproach us and lay our want of success to this cause.

There are however considerations on the other side. Missionaries are men as well as others. They have sometimes fallen prey to licentiousness among the heathen. Wives are a protection against this. Then women have been found as serviceable to the foreign field as men. And a weighty consideration is that by marrying, the missionary affords the heathen a model of a Christian family. We cannot lay down any fixed rule here, either in regard to the minister or missionary. Sometimes it may be better

Lecture Five

to remain unmarried. Paul leaves the question undecided, or for each one to decide for himself. All depends upon a man's circumstances and upon his constitutional character. If this permit him, and he think that he can do more good by remaining unmarried, he ought to do so. There is no merit in celibacy as such, and this is the point of Catholic error. So also poverty for the glory of God has merit, but not as such.

A missionary should have special compassion for the heathen; and this should be steady and permanent, not fitful or fanciful. Young men are very apt to have such starts. Yet the hollowness of such feeling appears from their having no heart for the poor negro at his door. This is a proper test whether our missionary feeling is romantic and sentimental merely, or real and genuine.

The leading of Providence should here be looked to as in other cases. Here proper judgment is necessary; for Providence may at first obstruct for the sake of trying him. When these obstructions are removed, the call stands out more clear to his mind. There may be inseparable objections—the claims of society at home, &c. that he cannot go. The judgment of friends is no good reason against going abroad, if other things indicate a call.

Supposing the question to be settled that a man is to stay at home, the question next arises, to what particular church or charge shall he go? Here also God must call him to his proper field, not in a supernatural way, but by his Spirit and providence. It is thought that people should have the right to call men, yet the right is not so very clear and palpable. It is very questionable in the end, whether it tends to give us the best pastoral relations. The New Testament is not very clear on this point. In the progress of time, the right fell almost altogether into the hands of the bishops. It is not clear from the modern practice that it is the best way. The danger of distractions and parties is very great. In many places the people are altogether unfit to choose a pastor. Patronage is also an evil. Here the power of choosing is not in the ecclesiastical power, but in an individual lay member. The contest on this point has lately led to the Scotch Secession.

The meaning of *license* is that the ecclesiastical power has the right of judging whether a man shall be a candidate for the ministry or not. A licentiate is no minister, but only a candidate. The Classes say who shall be candidates, and then determine afterwards whether the call shall be confirmed or not. The principle is that the people must be satisfied. It is only a veto power.

The question of settlement should be treated with prayer, earnestly and with a strict regard to the will of God, rather than self-will. He should not push himself forward but follow rather as God may lead. When the way is open, let him preach on trial. But let him avoid being in the pulpit more than he is habitually. The case calls for fair dealing. Court not popularity. Do not even cherish a wish to be settled in a particular place, but wait on God. If his being a candidate threatens a division, let him at once withdraw. This does not mean that he should yield to every position. He may yield as a minority. Encourage no hope in a church where you cannot become its pastor.

There must be no such thing as ministerial coquetry—courting calls to flatter his vanity. This is ever more contemptible than in the case of females. When called, he must seek direction by prayer and not be too hasty to accept. The advice of friends is not much to be regarded. Settlement among kindred is not very desirable. He may then be led to partiality, and is thus placed in peculiar difficulties. He may be charged with it, where he is not— then to avoid it he may be partial against his friends.

Trust not in first appearances. These are often very deceptive. He should use the cunning of a serpent with the harmlessness of the dove. A congregation may put on a very favorable countenance. He ought to be very cautious where he does not know the men. Those who promise most, may be the last to be depended on. Hence he should not trust first appearance, either *against or for himself.*

At this point he is also required to meet and settle the question of support. This should be understood before hand. He should be relieved from all temporal embarrassment for the sake of the ministry itself. Thus there can be nothing wrong in exercising prudence here. It will often save both parties from difficulties. He may make sacrifices for there may be some charges which cannot give him a sufficient support; but where a people are able to give a proper support, he has no right to settle among them without such provision.

Preaching

This had its origin in the synagogue worship, not in the temple. Has two parts, 1. Matter of preaching and 2. Manner of preaching.

1. Matter of preaching. This is the Word.
- He must not preach self to be seen and admired of men.
- Not opinions and fancies of men; it is fearful to trifle with divine things.
- Not vain mixtures of philosophy—a source of mischief in the pulpit, in all ages.
- Not to reject by this all philosophy, for this is necessary to a proper understanding of Scriptures; but we must not make the Word lead to philosophy.
- Not metaphysics in the American sense of the term—they confound and inflate, rather than edify.
- It should not be controversial—this distracts; but it should be positive. Such an exposition of truth overthrows error.
- He should not preach politics. Yet this does not say that he should neglect the good of his country. It is altogether right that he should enforce national duties; yet he must not throw himself into the whirlpool of party politics. The spirit of party is never the spirit of Christianity.
- Not minute, verbal criticism—results, not apparatus and process should appear.

The Bible is the ground of all right preaching. It should be studied, and much of it committed to memory, so as to have facility in quoting scripture. This will give force to his words,

The Reformed Pastor

when done pertinently. Committing should be done in youth. Hard to do it afterwards. Boyhood is the best time. The Waldenses made much account of this. Required them to know Paul's epistles by heart. Well to have it so—also the Psalms.

All truths of the Bible should be preached in their proper relations and proportions;
- God and his attributes—his relations to men.
- The law, just, reasonable, good, unchangeable, indispensable—its use before and since the fall.
- Sin and guilt, as revealed by the Law.
- Christ and his Cross—the Alpha and Omega of the Gospel. We have already seen what it is to preach Christ (see notes on homiletics).
- The Trinity
- Grace and election
- Faith
- Work of the Spirit
- The Christian life—not merely moral, but flowing inwardly and outwardly from Christ.

Be familiar with experience. Be not overstrained or lax. Be clear, not vague, or general, yet not too nice and minute. There is a loose latitudinarian spirit of preaching which does not reach the conscience; and there is an opposite extreme, just as bad, where every duty is presented in too high wrought a form where everything becomes unreal, because of too high tension. Young men frequently fall into this way and wonder why their preaching has little effect. This kind of preaching is not the result of a calm and steady faith. The Gospel is calm and should be presented calmly. It is a great matter to see and pursue the right course—to treat Christianity as a system of life. The preacher should be clear, not vague, life must be presented as a reality. Social and relative duties. Final judgment. Errors must be opposed didactically, as occasions turn up. Vice must be rebuked with meekness, not human wrath. The Bible should be the main source of illustrations also.

Lecture Six

Manner of Preaching

Respect must be had not only to the matter, but also to the manner. Here there must be:
1. *Sincerity*. This requires that he should be firmly grounded, not doubting or wavering; that he should be firmly rooted in the divine life. It is of immense account to his own comfort also, that he should be free from all skeptical doubt. In such a case the mind becomes barren and unfruitful. It is indispensable to the power of truth also as exercised on others: truth must come from a living power, or else it has no force. If the truth which the word represents is not present, the word is dead. It is not possible to give living power to words that do not proceed from life. A man may be consumed to produce an effect, but it is of no account. Mere natural convictions of Christianity are not enough therefore. Sincerity, then, is a requisite of the first importance.
2. *Instructive*. Not loose declarations, nor flourishes of rhetoric. Doctrinal, experimental and practical. Simple and plain for the many, not for the few. It should be system-

atic. Here there is a great defect in our modern preaching, particularly where the minister chooses his own texts; church lessons being rejected. He is apt to choose the subject which falls in best with the state of his own mind. The other plan is better and easier in the end, to follow some course, or the catechism, or Apostles' Creed.

3. *It ought to be scriptural.* He should follow some order in this. Not abstract, but rather in the way of illustration. Expository preaching, rightly conducted, is the most profitable, but at the same time the most difficult. The reason why this kind of preaching is so little attended to is that it is so difficult. Good expository preaching would be more interesting than mere sermonizing. Henry's Commentary is valuable as a continued expository sermon. So Leighton, commenting on Peter: this is full of thought.

4. *The preaching should be affectionate.* Earnestness and compassion should appear in language, looks, and in his whole manner. Everything contrary would be a defect. Hence his preaching should not be flippant or foppish, for this implies a want of affection. It should not be *cold or heartless*, which shows itself in an angry denunciatory style. This often disguises itself under a show of zeal for the interest of God—but in such cases the motives are after all selfish: it turns upon himself and has no reference to God. He is angry because *he* cannot move the people. He thinks himself the great power of God—is disappointed, his pride wounded, and complains of their hardness and blindness, simply because they will not yield. Often the hortatory part of a sermon is actuated by such a spirit, but it is the wrath of man, and not the power of God. There must be real tenderness, and this is not put on or assumed, but is the overflow of the inmost soul. Nor is a general natural tenderness sufficient; it must flow from faith. It is the fruit of deep piety.

5. It should be *Evangelical*—Christ and his Cross. The pure gospel, as a system of life. This requires that he should

Lecture Six

understand and present evangelical motives, not legal or moral merely. Evangelical motives do not consist in merely ringing changes on Christ and the Gospel. If their appeal is to the lowest principles in men, to their fears or interests, or want of consistency, then their preaching is not evangelical, but legal. Our preaching is very defective here, when compared with the Epistles. Paul's motives are mostly drawn from the privileges, hopes, and glory of the church and its glory. Ministers generally think that such motives are only for a high state of religion, and that their congregations are not prepared for them. But this is gospel preaching indeed. Archbishop Leighton always uses such motives, and we can feel their power.

6. *It should be with authority*—not dogmatically, but as an ambassador for Christ. To preach with real authority the minister requires holy boldness. He stands in the pulpit not to argue or dispute, but to *testify* as a witness for God—not in his own name simply, but in the name of the congregation whose organ he is; and if he preach as in a debating society, he disgraces his office.
7. *It should be with discrimination*—having respect to the converted and unconverted—the growing and the backsliding—suitable to different classes. Not of uncertain sound.
8. *It should be with impartiality*—know no man after the flesh. Avoid flattery and connivance at sin. This does not require to be coarse or offensive. Preach the truth, affect whom it may, others or self.
9. *He should preach comprehensively and harmoniously.* The whole truth, in its order and place, the connections and relations.
10. *He should preach diligently.* Neglect not the work that is in thee. The minister is not his own, in time, talents, or pursuits; but is bound to use his power as he best may to the glory of God. To misemploy them or himself is sacrilege. His office is a work, not a mere business. Here the ques-

tion may arise, how often should a minister preach? As often as strength and opportunity allows, where there are any prospects of doing good. Some may be able to preach more frequently than others. There is need here of great prudence and caution. Some persons keep a record of all the sermons they preach, as if this were indicative of the good they did. The good a minister does, depends not on the quantity but on the quality of preaching. Preaching is not the only worth of a pastor. Too frequently preaching, while it will keep him from proper attendance upon his other duties, will also prevent him from proper preparation. The idea of preaching requires that there should be preparation, and he will be preaching to little purpose without. In such a case as Whitfield, there may be said to have been a particular call. But even he did not preach a different sermon each time.

11. *He must preach with fidelity* which includes all faithfulness to God and the people, watching for souls, & c. Sermons should be prepared and watered with tears.

In regard to extemporaneous preaching and the use of notes, nothing can be settled in an absolute way. Off hand efforts should be avoided. Let there be preparation. Different methods suit different men. The feelings of the people also should be consulted. Where these are against written sermons, he ought to do without. As a general thing, the minister should not have his manuscript before him to read. The proper idea of preaching would seem to demand this. Nor can any absolute rule be laid down with reference to writing and committing to memory. It is better where a man will not be at the mercy of his notes. It will be more apt to have an excellent effect. There are cases in which it would be better to commit or even to read. Either of these may be cultivated to a great extent. A man should not hastily determine which will be best for him. He should observe and then cultivate that method which suits him best, and which he can obtain.

Lecture Six

Extemporizing is most difficult, and a young minister should not trust himself absolutely to it from the very start. If he thinks he can succeed in it, he ought to cultivate it in connection with his other preparation. Then to assist him, it will be of great importance to cultivate a proper and natural style, one that falls in with his manner of thinking. Hence he should not fall into a high flown style, for this becomes to him a law from which he cannot escape. In proportion as this is artificial it will become difficult for him to move. Hence our style should be direct, not that we should bring our writing down to our conversational style, but to receive the latter to some extent, and enable it.

1. Keep in view always the end of preaching - the glory of God and the salvation of men.
2. Cultivate a deep sense of personal insufficiency.
3. Pray much for divine blessings before and after your sermon.
4. Be diligent in preparing, but lean not presumptuously upon it, and then throw yourself on God, as though unprepared.
5. Study the character of the people.
6. Labor to gain and hold attention.
7. Be affectionate, yet always discriminating, pungent and powerful.
8. Be in appearance grave, modest, kind, & c.
9. Grow not weary in preaching.
10. Seek to be made free from the fear of man, which proceeds most from pride.

Catechism

This is the second general department of the pastoral work. It has reference chiefly to the young, though not exclusively. The young have a special claim upon the minister. They form the hope of the church - the life of the church prospectively considered belongs to the young: whilst the old are passing away, they must be marshaled to the ranks; and if the minister neglects them, the church must necessarily decline. Then the young in themselves form a more favorable field than the old for the ministerial work. Their character is just forming—are more open—and hence special promises to them in the scripture. The labor expended upon them always meets with a rich reward.

Then the church is educational in her very constitution. The plan here is that the human race from its birth should be taken up into the new life. The church, as a supernatural institution, includes powers to this effect. The ministry is under a wrong view, where it has come to think otherwise. Hence, the education of the young may be said to belong to the missionary work, and none is more important than this. It is a sad state when the church allows herself to neglect this, whilst she contributes to foreign labor. Hence men most eminent and successful have always paid special attention to the young. Baxter. Doddridge.

Catechetical instruction is not, however, to be confined to the young. In many churches there are many of mature years who would be vastly profited by it. It is particularly adapted to those whose style of thinking is plain and childlike, whether young or old. There are large classes of people who need this kind of instruction, and would be profited by this, if conducted rightly, even more than by preaching: not indeed to the exclusion of the latter, but in connection with it. So the colored population, and also most common people. Sometimes whole churches have been formed into a class with very good effect. In the time of the Reformation a very large amount of religious instruction was disseminated in this form. Many classes were formed and the people took great interest in it. Old and young flocked together. In Zurich there was a person specially appointed to attend to this department. So in most large cities in Switzerland. The work in this form is not the same as in the primitive church, but may be said to have commenced with the Reformation.

It should be conducted systematically according to the de-

Lecture Six

velopment of mind. First, historical truths—then elementary doctrines—then complete schemes. It is not to be conducted by the ministry only, but also by parents and all qualified persons. It belongs to the duty of the church as such. In the family it should commence as soon as the child begins to speak, and where it is not commenced here, it will not have much force afterwards. The domestic instruction in this case, indeed, is to be considered as the instruction of the church.

It should be carried on in schools. Schools are in connection with the church, and stand under its supervision. Teachers and teaching should always be religious. This idea has been carried out more fully in Europe. An attempt has been made in the Presbyterian church to revive the custom. It is a gross schism in a Christian country to employ infidel teachers. Teachers are functionaries of the church, just as parents are. Hence catechetical instruction ought to be kept up in the schools.

The work, of course, belongs to the pastor too, though he may employ elders or others properly qualified. It ought to be frequent to meet its end, and he should oversee and regulate the whole. This requires system and plan. It is important also to have stated examinations publicly, at which the pastor should be present. Parents should be exhorted to attend with their children. This was customary in the Presbyterian church some time back, though now it has fallen into disuse. It was in order to keep up the custom at home, for at these examinations it would come to light whether it had been attended to. This whole system was got up in the 16th century and it wrought wonders. In Switzerland, Holland, and the Palatinate, it is still in use.

Candidates for the Lord's Supper should be catechized specially—not merely to try them but to instruct. This is in accordance with the custom of the early church. So now they should be called upon to give an account of their faith. We can have no set length of time. If very ignorant, let them be held long as catechumens: until they are prepared to make confession of faith. This very training is in itself a means of grace. In the case of persons who cannot read, or have learned late, this system is all important. We think first by the ear, rather than by the eyes. So ignorant persons generally read aloud. For the same reason preaching is so effectual. The sense of hearing is more internal than that of sight. With such ignorant persons instruction must be plain, reiterating and patient. The minister must lower himself to them, rather than force them up to him. Hasty admissions are to be deprecated.

Young baptized persons should be looked upon as they grow up, as candidates for communion, whether they consider themselves to be such or not. They are bound to come forward at the proper time and form a catechetical class. The church should insist upon it, and they should he disciplined if they refuse to submit to the authority of the church. It is a great evil that this should be neglected in this country. These look upon connection with the church as first established at profession. This is selling one's birthright. It is a great advantage that this system holds in the case of the German churches in this country.

Confirmation is no sacrament, but the completion of the rite of baptism. With this it was connected at first, but separated when baptism passed into the hands of the presbyters, and confirmation was retained by the bishops. When these could not be present, it was deferred to a convenient season. Afterwards, what had at first been an exception, became a standing rule. In the Reformed church it fell into disuse at first, but was afterwards revived and kept up. Calvin expresses his regret that it was not kept up.

There can be no valid objection to this ceremony although some consider it as Romanizing. For in the nature of the case a personal profession of faith is necessary in the case of the baptized at sometime, and the church must look to it that it is made, and that baptism is not disregarded. Baptists and others object to it being made in this methodic style, and say that we should wait until the Spirit of God urges them. But here the error is wholly on the Baptist side. The baptized are the property of the church, its members, and they are not to be left to their wills. The church is bound to call upon them, to see whether they are

Lecture Six

willing to take on them the cross. There can be no objection to this methodic way. Indeed we must have some ceremony and we cannot do without it. The most subjective of our churches place the most on these forms. In New England, where they protest against confirmation, they require them to come forward in the church, and make a covenant with the church. It is no objection to say that the system has been abused, any other may be abused. Some method of instruction must be used, and thus laying on of hands in confirmation, being of Apostolic origin, is the best and most appropriate. Here both in matter and in forms there is no rational objective to confirmation. In any right view, it must be looked upon as a very important institution, and it should be kept up. Whenever this has fallen into disuse, the proper idea of baptism has almost inevitably been lost; and it is one of the greatest evils in the church and this country, that owing to the Methodistic and Baptistic principles, this has been lost: that the relation existing between the church and the baptized has been forgotten.

We admit that the system has been abused: that is has often been suffered to sink to a dead form. But so may any system of profession. It is still one of immense power. It brings the young directly under pastoral care. It forms a solemn *call* to piety. This is of great advantage to the minister. There is no difficulty in inducing children to come, and the parents feel it right to send them. What opportunity fairer for dealing with conscience? Let the pastor *feel* the weight of the case. Let him be earnest, affectionate, thorough. If it proves a form, it is *his* fault. If we had a proper ministry, we would soon see the power of the system. He must see the state of the heart, and life, as well as knowledge. Much piety is needed to proceed properly in the duty—faithful and patient.

Above the catechetical class comes what is generally called the Bible Class. Very important also. It fills up, in some degree, the void between childhood and manhood. They should include if possible, however, adults also. It forms a good substitute for an afternoon service, if well managed. Here the minister should remember, however, that the object is not so much to draw out knowledge as to engage attention. Sometimes the minister defeats his object by asking too hard questions. Hence they should be plain and simple: so constructed as to engage interest.

Belonging to the same system is the Sunday School. It is important to parents, children and teachers. The system is somewhat liable to run into abuse. The instruction should be biblical and practical. Be carried on with reference to catechism. Classes should be small. The minister cannot always be present, but should be so frequently at the close of the hour, and should oversee the whole system. It should be part of the church.

The Sunday School should not be looked upon as a substitute for family instruction. Hence discipline is indispensable. The necessity and desirableness of Sunday School arises from the fact that there are so many parents who are utterly incompetent to teach their children. The church in such cases should take the education of their children out of their hands. But others should also send their children to encourage the system. Still, in no case does it put away with domestic instruction and discipline.

Ministers should try to gain the confidence of the young. He should cultivate such a spirit and conduct that they may feel that he takes an interest in them. Sometimes his influence is such that the young are repelled. This is his fault. Children are not easily deceived in this case. They have a sort of infallible instinct to decide whether the minister feels any sympathy with them. He should hold himself to them so as to attract them to his person. As they grow up let them be encouraged to visit the parsonage.

In catechetical instruction, feel and show a lively interest. Try to make it interesting. Enlist helpers, elders, teachers, parents, etc. Discourage a spirit of contention and vain curiosity. Do not suffer the system to run out into worldly interest. Inculcate reverence and show it by example. Be diligent in preparing. Study character. Have patience.

Lecture Six

Visitation

Another part of the pastoral work is visitation. This is highly important for it brings the work of the pulpit into direct contact with the wants of the individual. It is necessary in addition to the more general service of the church. It requires the deepest and most fervent piety. In the pulpit mere eloquence may help him along, but here he needs more than this. It is recommended especially by Paul, both in word and example. See his address to the elders at Ephesus. He tends to conciliate confidence and affection: so that it is not only important as a private work, but tends also to increase interest in the public ministrations, and gives more pertinence to the preaching. In the case of the poor this is very important. They are very sensitive, and apt to think themselves, from their humble circumstances, overlooked. But this visitation will gain their confidence and make them look up to the pastor as an adviser and friend who sympathizes with them. The more intimate a minister is with the character, relations and circumstances of his congregation, the better. So Cyprian, Ignatius. It brings him to know the want of families. The pastoral relation ought to constitute the minister the general adviser of his congregation, even in secular affairs. This depends somewhat on the state of the congregation. A refined and intelligent congregation does not need it. Yet, in many, this part of his work is very important. The minister thus becomes a bosom friend, to whom they unburden their difficulties. He should, moreover, show a lively interest in their affairs and clothe himself with a paternal character. And just so far as he does this, will he have influence over them. We have a fine example here in Oberlin. It ought to be the general object of the pastor to promote the interests of his congregation, internally and externally, in secular as well as spiritual affairs. And all his zeal may well be suspected as being spurious, if he shows no regard to this. There are many cases in which he could obviate difficulties in families by his mere advice. In proportion as he is acquainted with their circumstances, he has direct opportunities of doing them good by advice and in other ways. Whereas without it, he would miss them, and thus lessen his influence. It enables him to give direct and particular instruction, which is highly important.

Pastoral visits should be exclusively religious, not social. This should be the prime and only object. Many ministers visit very often, and take to themselves the credit of being good pastors, whereas they are merely social, and do not reach their object at all. But they should be religious. It ought to be understood, and he ought to labor to make it thus, that his visits carry with them this character, and no other. Some give their visits a social character, in order to introduce religion by *stealth*. But he ought to make it be understood by all, that this is a part of his work, that when he comes, he comes on a spiritual errand. Then the way will always be open to private religious instruction. It will save much time and trouble, and give effect to his presence. His mere presence will constitute a sermon. The minister then should instruct his congregation from the pulpit, on this subject, and make it understood that the object of his visits is a spiritual one, and no other.

In connection with these visits there should always be *prayer*. It should be considered a religious service. There should be an endeavor to remove restraint, not by becoming secular, but by producing confidence in him as pastor. And the more they have this confidence in him as spiritual guide, the more unrestrained he will feel. He should have a deep concern for souls. Be faithful as watching for souls. Study wisdom and cultivate affection. Standing questions may answer a good purpose on such occasions. This saves lots of time, and it would be well if these were understood by families.

Visits should be as frequently as possible, at least once a year. Where it is impracticable to visit families in detail, as in cities, or widely scattered charges, several may be requested to meet at one place. Such visits may not be as unrestrained as where one family is visited alone, yet may be made to partake of the character of a pastoral visit. But they should not be looked upon as a prayer meeting. In our church charges are mostly too large.

In visiting, the minister should pass by no one falling properly within the congregation, whether church going or not. In every community there are families who go to no church. Such should be called upon, unless where it should be thought interfering with other churches, in which case, of course, he should stay away. Many are often induced thus to come to church, particularly the poor. Be ready to give good practical advice on all subjects.

This duty cannot be dispensed with. The talent for it (edifying conversation, & c.) should be cultivated. No one can excuse himself, thinking that he has not this talent. If the first part of the day has been given to study, the balance may well be given to practical work. The minister may study too much.

Visit of sick and afflicted

These form a special class for visitation. As the sick call for special sympathy, so he should pay the more attention to them: and the pastor cannot be faithful who allows himself to overlook them. He should look with a shepherd's eye on the weak and distressed.

"If any one is sick among you? Let him call for the elders of the church, and let them prayer over him, & c." Here the duty becomes more difficult than in ordinary visitation. Here he needs sympathy, wisdom, and prudence. His duty cannot be discharged artificially and mechanically. He needs to cultivate regard for divine things. The heart must have experience, full of faith in God's word, and an abiding sense of eternal things. This is what makes it so difficult. But the minister is called upon to live in the element of the Spirit and of faith: to be prepared to meet the sick with sympathy and counsel, be full of compassion and love, like Christ. Faithfulness, plain and earnest dealing, are loudly demanded here. It is fearful to tamper with souls in such a state. The object of his visit here is to turn the affections of the sick to spiritual things, not only in view of death, but also in view of restoration.

The people should be instructed from the pulpit to send for the minister in cases of sickness. He should make them feel that it is their duty to do so, and to do it *early*. Many think that the minister should not be sent for until the case becomes desperate, but this has an injurious effect in many ways. It confuses the patient—makes him think that he is worse than he really is. But he ought to be sent for even when there is no prospect of death: for the object of calling in the minister, and this should be distinctly understood, is not to prepare him for death, but to turn the visitation to spiritual account, whether he live or die.

When called upon the minister should be ready always to go, at any hour day or night. He should regard this as part of his official duty, binding him to go, just as much as the physician. The minister should not wait until he is sent for, if he hears of sickness. He should even go if he has reason to suppose that the friends do not wish it: for his visit is not for the friends, but for the sick person. If they absolutely prevent him, he stands acquitted.

He should teach the people the folly and sin of trying to keep the sick from religious instruction and conversation. Friends sometimes in order to save their own feelings are not willing that he should be called in. It seems to make the case desperate and they do not wish to excite the patient. Hence he should take pains to instruct them on this point, even when there is some danger, his visits should be allowed to sick persons in view of an interest that is higher than that of his bodily life. But the instruction needs to go still further. It is a mere prejudice to suppose that the visit of the minister will be attended with harm to the sick person, and this goes on the assumption that the mind of the person will not be drawn in the direction of death, unless an outward occasion is afforded him. Yet this is not the case. The mind here is not in a stupor, and the presumption is that he will be more tuned to these subjects. Then the friends may be reserved, or even have no sympathy with religious subjects, so that he cannot unbosom himself, and his feelings are kept pent up within himself, which will be more dangerous than a pastoral visit, when he can have an opportunity of unburdening himself, which will always be a great relief. It is much more dangerous not to do this than to have free conversation with the minister. This brings himself in the sphere of sympathy, which in itself will be healthful. There are very few cases in which a pastoral visit will be injurious to a sick person; generally they are conducive to health. Even when the visits of indifferent persons are not allowed, it is good in case of the minister. The pastor, however, may be reserved and difficult, and prove irksome to the sick. This is very bad. Most sick are anxious about spiritual points, and find relief in conversing of them. He then ought to try and enter into their feelings with them, so that his presence may surround them with a healthful atmosphere.

In visiting the sick the minister should labor fully to know the case he may have in hand. He should be direct and pointed, speaking to the conscience, with love and fidelity. He should encourage the sick to unburden their hearts by a full and free confession. This is often of vital account—affords great relief and he should encourage him to do it. It often happens that a secret sin of several years standing, in health kept down, now rises up to trouble his conscience. It is all important that this sin should be brought out. This one point is often *vital*. He can do nothing if this be not done. The patient should reveal it to be clear with himself. The minister is bound to professional secrecy, in such a case, of course, like the lawyer or physician. And this ought to be understood that the bosom of the minister is an inviolable sanctuary.

Let known sins of omission or commission be faithfully pressed. The minister should be prudent and cautious. Have respect to the body, as well as the soul. He should spare no error or delusion. Cry not peace where there is no peace, but deal tenderly and with judgment. The minister should understand the proper state of the malady, and meet it as it is. It may be ignorance—then simple instruction may do much. It may be stupidity—then call and arouse. It may be false hopes—then shake them and lead him to others substantial and firm. Have ready the proper remedy for every case, convincing of sin and leading to Jesus.

Be not vague and tedious, in the form of the homily. Scepticism is best overcome generally by select portions of the Bible itself read, rather than by argument. He should exhort the sick to arrange their worldly affairs. This should be done early to prevent future difficulties—also for the sake of the sick himself. This duty should be off the mind. If it be not, he will shrink of it, and it will trouble him. He may become worse, when he will be altogether unfit for it.

In the worst cases the minister should not give up, just as in the case of the physician. Some word of truth may still take effect. Prayer here calls for lively feeling and wisdom. It is particularly difficult. They are apt to become too long and even tedious—the mind of the sick becomes weary and cannot follow him. They should therefore be short, full of faith, full of point, and appropriate, very *simple*, consisting of short sentences and single petitions. The sick should be taught to offer up ejaculatory prayer; such are often of more account than any other. And these, at last are the only ones that can be offered up.

Then the minister should labor to benefit attending friends, & c. When the sick may be out of reach, good can still be done for others. The occasion can thus be turned to important account for families. Condemned criminals should also be visited. The treatment of their case is the same, yet the advantage of health is there.

In the case of the *Pestilence*, the duty becomes still more arduous and attended with danger. Yet the pastor must stay at his post and he dare not fly from it, for visiting the sick is just as much his duty as it is the duty of the physician. There may be circumstances in which the duty may not hold: as when there is no room to hope for good by his presence, and where the prospect of death is certain. But the minister generally has no right to retract from his duty. Catholics have often reproached Protestants, that its ministers have been ready to fly in case of cholera and yellow fever. It must be granted that the Catholic priesthood and Sisters of Charity have been very faithful in such cases, and show a fine example in this respect.

Visitation of the Poor

In visitation to the *poor,* particular attention must be paid. These were especially regarded by the Gospel in all ages. "To the poor the Gospel is preached." This is a peculiarity of the Christian system. Ancient philosophical schools paid no respect to them. But Christianity is peculiarly adapted to them. Hence the minister must have special regard to these. The man who allows himself to overlook the poor habitually shows that he is not qualified for his station. The *poor need* instruction; they have not the same opportunities; they are not able to take in knowledge by reading; they are generally more disposed to *receive* instruction than others. Kindness here tells with more effect than in any other classes. Hence pastoral visitation among the poor is an important means to do good, to secure influence, and establish him in his charge. This is more important than their visitation among the rich. The children of God are chiefly among the poor.

More is however required than mere visiting. The pastor should show liberality to the poor, however small the gifts may be on account of narrow circumstances. They produce a large return of gratitude, love, &c. The smallness of his salary should form no excuse for withholding such. If a man's liberality all runs abroad, and neglects the poor around him, he does not do his duty. Liberality at home is of far more account, for the value of the gift must not be measured by its amount abstractly, but by the moral good it may do. Besides the minister must stir up his congregation to relieve the poor. He should consider himself the general supervisor of this. The elders must help him in this, and he must infuse into them the spirit.

The church as such is bound to make provision for her poor. They are members of the same body. This very image implies that care must be taken of poor members. This does not require a community of goods, but a community of life. The rich are bound to use their goods for the benefit of the whole, not for their own benefit merely. The church in the beginning felt this duty. Weekly contributions were made, one third of which were appropriated to the poor. So in the first centuries, amid all the persecutions, the poor were well attended to. But not only was care taken of the poor in their own congregation, but those of others also, and even of the heathen poor. Thus Christianity stood in favorable contrast with heathenism. After Christianity became to prevail, this taking care of the poor was undertaken by the State; yet this cannot absolve the church from her duty. It is a bad arrangement, and it has now become a question, whether such legislative support is to be advocated by the Christian, or not. For though good in itself, it has suspended a better form, for, as has been already remarked, the value of the donation is not to be measured by the relief it gives to the poor, but the moral relation it establishes between the *giver* and the *receiver*. It calls up benevolence on the one side, gratitude on the other; very important in the Christian economy. "The poor you have always with you," implying that they belong to the church. If there were no poor, a particular development of the Christian life would be taken away. So if the parental relation were taken away. So the relation between the poor and the rich forms a part of the Christian economy; and it does injury both to the rich and the poor if this relation is destroyed. If the State take care of them, their support is levied in the form of a tax; in paying this no room is left for Christian benevolence and charity, for the tax is looked upon as an exaction. Then the poor are also not affected as they would be in the case of personal charity. The gift is not received with gratitude, for the pauper looks upon it as his right; he becomes idle, unthrifty, and vicious often, and looks upon the rich with anger and envy. State provision, then, can never answer the purpose; as it neutralizes the moral benefit of charity both to

Lecture Six

the giver and receiver. Pauperism is a great evil, as exemplified in England. Their self respect is gone, and they are willing to be thrown on the system. This is Pauperism, not poverty. No system is good, if it does not lead to self respect. In England the Pauperism leads to no moral result. Dr. Chalmers has written extensively and ably on this subject. He opposes the English system and its introduction into Scotland altogether. He goes to show that the poor are much better taken care of by the church. He made a successful experiment of this in Glasgow. In such case there will not be half the number of paupers. The poor will practice more economy. The condition of the poor in Scotland is much better than that of the poor in England, particularly when these are taken care of by the church. See Dr. Chalmers *Civil and Political Economy*. The church *suffers* when the poor are taken off her hands. Charity, to be effective, must be particular and personal, not general, by wholesale or by proxy. It cannot be taken from the church and given to the State: just as the family education cannot be transferred to the Sabbath School. It is a part of the Christian economy.

The pastor should labor to suppress pauperism. Where the poor are kept within the church, poverty cannot become prevalent. It is only when they are overlooked and treated as animals that they look also upon themselves as such and become willing to become paupers. The minister then must instill proper feelings with regard to it and withstand its causes. Especially must he oppose intemperance in its root and ground. On the same principle he should promote industry, and he has the power to do it. Charity that encourages idleness is hurtful.

Let, then, comfortable provision be made in the house of God. This is a great safe guard. They should feel that they also belong to the body of Christ and should not be thrust out either directly or indirectly, which is the case when churches are so constructed that they are frightened out of it. This is a great evil in Protestant denominations. The Methodists have done away with it in their free churches, in which they have a great advantage over the others. The poor generally form the strength of the community. Pains should be taken to bring them into the church. They must be looked after and encouraged with regard to this point, and it should not be felt that the congregation is indifferent with regard to their coming. The minister has it in his power to do much here. Any church that neglects the poor, cannot flourish. It must be admitted that the Roman Catholic Church has, in her own way, surpassed the Protestants here. They always had an eye to the poor, and make much account of them. Their churches are free, and their whole system has much account for the poor. More account was paid to the poor in England before than after the Reformation.

The minister should condescend to the poor, not affectedly, seemingly taking an interest in them; but he should have the spirit of condescension; attend to little things; put away fastidiousness; be at home in their company. He should try to promote neatness, cleanliness, order, & c. in their houses. This is highly important to their comfort and religion most effectually serves this end. No Christian community can neglect this. There is a close connection between outward and inward cleanliness. Religion and cleanliness promote each other mutually. Hence the minister should not consider it beneath him to attend to this.

He should discountenance all extravagance among them, frolics, & c. which are here more hurtful than among the rich. Oberlin exerted an immense influence in his rude parish in this way, internally and externally. He raised his rough mountaineers. They were all poor, and he was poor too. But he promoted economy, neatness, & c. The Roman Catholic missionaries have always had an eye to this. Let then the minister have this condescension. He should endeavor to raise the community in all respects. Let all attention proceed from the spirit of the Gospel (love) without affectation.

Visitation of the Awakened

The *awakened* form another class which demand special attention. It should be taken for granted that there are always such

Lecture Six

persons in his congregation, and he should not think that they are to be found only during commotions. Wherever the gospel is preached faithfully, there is always an inquiring party, especially among the young, holding a middle position between the obedient and the callous. They should be regarded as a standing class. His eye should be upon them. To guide convicted persons is most important and most difficult. They are in a crisis. Mere excitement must be distinguished from conviction. There may be the former where the latter is wanting, and there may be conviction without commotion or excitement. The temperament of the individual must be looked to. These utter themselves in the same state in different ways. The same amount of conviction may be expressed much more strongly in one case than in the other. Sympathy in times of revival is very great and hard to understand. Hasty opinions of the state of *awakened* persons should not be expressed. They are not at all necessary, and are in most cases uncertain and dangerous. The errors of the awakened should be discovered, and if possible removed in private.

Revivals are to be desired and sought; the reality of them is not to be questioned. There are periods when the Spirit of God takes advantage of the common sympathies of men to promote religion. Yet occasions of this kind are to be tried. Many false revivals have been abroad. To *encourage* every excitement as a *revival* is insane. Vast injury is done to religion where this spirit, compounding excitement with revival, prevails.

New measures in general are wrong—indicate quackery, dependance on form more than spirit. Anxious seats and other decision acts betray shallow conceptions of religion. The whole theory of religious instruction at the anxious seat is unphilosophical. Indeed instruction to the awakened is not at all aided by this process. Better to address altogether, than two or three words in detail. The faithful exhibition of God's truth is the best means of leading such to repentance. Serious and awakened persons are in danger 1st. of losing their impressions by new things, change, temptation, outward reformation, false hopes, reaction,

& c. Any state of excitement will reach a crisis, when a reaction will take place, which will give relief from previous tension of feelings; this state is quite different from the former. This is mistaken for conversion, because they have looked for conversion in this way. But it is a false one, a mere delusion. It is marvelous that men are so blind to so natural a danger. 2nd. Of slight healing and false peace—by external reform, religious duties, sympathetic affections; in great distress a mere burst of tears may bring animal composure; joy may burst on the soul, unaccountably without any spiritual view of truth. 3rd. Enthusiasm—arising from mere feeling—wild at first, it ends often on some other fatal evil, of a contrary from; Anabaptists, Quakers, and work in the West. 4th. Despair—results generally of presumptuous sins under awakening. Against all such danger the minister must guard.

Instruction to the awakened should be simple, turning them from vain inquiry, controversial points. Guard against fretful impatience. Hold up the truth. Be discriminating. Recommend suitable books, particularly the Bible. Warn against vain confidence and pride.

Children should not be admitted to the Lord's Supper before 12 years old—the time when children were admitted to the Jewish Passover. Old candidates should be well instructed. Act not on the principle that an excitement must soon pass over. This is generally done, but is a wrong feeling. Deprecate the coldness too often consequent on such seasons.

Persons in darkness need particular attention and sympathy. A melancholy temperament generally prevails with such. This bears no argument. The disease should be studied physiologically. The minister should be acquainted with the relation of the body to the soul; should know the temperament. Religion does not create melancholy, but melancholy turns naturally towards it. This ignorant persons will charge religion with. This is treated under this view by Rush and Dorsey particularly.

Anxious seats have become so common in some sections as no longer to seem included in the system of New Measures. But they belong to this system in fact, and form the opening wedge

Lecture Six

for all else it includes. At this time, the usage is carrying all before it in the Lutheran churches. This popularity and success is no argument in its favor. After all it is a stale, cast off device, of which other sections of the church have grown ashamed. So in New England and in the Presbyterian churches generally. Case of northern New York, scattered by Finneyism, and only slowly recovering now.

Immediate visible effects offer no argument in its favor. Conversion *may* be secured in this way. But the most false methods may lead to conversions in some cases: monkery, Stylitism, popish solemn pomp. Effect mainly theatrical and earthly. Often great after the most dull preaching. Wrought by appeals to fancy, fear, false judgment. Young persons, females, & c. its first subjects. In no connection with the true *spiritual* power in the preacher. Hence the sport of quacks and imposters, Campbellites, Universalists, Millerites, & c.

It is not an exercise of power, but of weakness. A quack must work not by the true virtue of things, but by legerdemain tricks to raise wonder. Attention in this form is of little account in religion. We need no *new* forms to rouse interest—but only that old forms be made to live. This is true strength. Old methods rightly used are mightier towards God than novelties, however striking. If a man cannot preach with effect, create interest, & c. without anxious seats, he shows himself to be spiritually weak. It is the result of quacks, novices, & c.

The system is wrong, as tending to direct the care of preaching from a more "excellent way," sheltering the weakness of weak men, puffing up novices, & c. The semblance of power in this way is easy to be reached—hence sought. "Royal road" to success and credit. Many a young man has been in this way spoiled for the ministry for life.

It is wrong as fostering false views of religion among the people. Theatrical excitement made to stand for religious feeling. Machinery exalted above instruction. A community subjected to such a process for some time loses its susceptibility for true spiritual cultivation.

The system is spiritually dangerous. 1st. It carries a false issue for the conscience. 2nd. It disturbs and distracts the truly serious spirit—causing outward relations to force the inward out of view. A young girl called to rise and pass through a great congregation, consciously in the eye of all, amid stirring excitement—how distracting, how killing to a calm deep reflection; exactly suited to strangle serious impressions in their birth. 3rd. It is liable to be regarded and rested in as a decision act in favor of religion, which it is not in fact. In some cases, the preacher may honestly guard against this, but generally not. Excitement rules the hour, and he calls to the anxious seat as to the cross of Christ itself. To refuse is made sin. Appeals are repeated. "Come humble sinner," & c. are sung. Then exhorted perhaps to go on as they have now begun. I have never witnessed the measures where room was not given for this censure. 4th. It leads to forced and rash committals. Nothing gained by these. Often the case of issuing in a false profession, or desperate breaking away from the means of grace. Anxious seat submission of the most questionable characters always. The system leads to disorder—opens the way to offer measures more offensive—connects itself naturally with a rude vulgar style in the house of God. Anecdotes. Personalty. Denunciation.

It accomplishes no good object to compensate for these evils. Vindicated on variable grounds, alike unsatisfactory. As a *decision* act, it decides nothing—brings no soul nearer to God. Gives no help for *instruction*. This must be general or particular, in the case. The last form sheer shooting at random in the dark—spectacle ridiculous. Only rational mode to exhort the "seat" collectively. But the same instruction could be given without the "seat," with full as much advantage. It helps not prayer in behalf of the serious—creates indeed often an element unfavorable to earnest prayer. True object is excitement and committal. The *coming* is itself the great end.

All purposes professedly sought in this way much better secured in other ways. Inquirers meetings—nothing lost ordinarily by waiting for time and place, even till next day. Pastoral visita-

Lecture Six

tion. Catechetical class. Rather have 50 in a catechetical class than 50 on an anxious seat. Ministers here have no right to bring in such a test, at their pleasure. No end to it, if the principle is admitted.

Promotion of Peace

The pastor should live above others, as their light and guide. Beware of making the views of the people your standard. Yield not to the common current of religious feeling. The minister must live for others in this respect, seeking to raise them higher and higher. Let him stir up others to be co-workers, especially his elders. Let him meet often with his elders, for improvement in piety and conversation on the interests of the congregation. Let him be jealous of things of dubious character, not positively wrong, but hurtful to the interests of piety in their tendency. Encourage religious meetings. The best security for peace in a congregation, is the power of religion actively prevailing. Warn much against tongue sins, slander, scandal, & c. Exhort to the suppression of angry passions and bad tempers, pride, avarice, religious controversy.

Where quarrels rise in the congregation, have no part in them, nor let any of your family take side with either party. Let not every difficulty come before the consistory, but use rather other methods first. See that the Gospel steps are taken by the plaintiff. Let not discipline be exercised without good reasons. Small offences call for private admonition, not public trial and censure. Let discipline be administered that it may be impressive and salutary.

Enemies

Beware of giving real occasion for enmity by imprudence or rashness. Avoid the spirit of ridicule and sarcasm, repulsive manners, harsh demeanor, morose tempers. Beware of conceiving a spirit of opposition towards known enemies or giving the smallest provocation for their dislike. Do good to those that hate you. Improve their enmity as a means of grace, a wholesome trial for patience, meekness, trust in God. It may bring to view real faults, not otherwise seen. If a pastor falls under the general dislike of his congregation, it is reason for him to withdraw. Let conscience, power, not passion, rule the step. Cultivate a holy life and blameless walk. Under persecutions take refuge in God, by prayer and reading the Bible, especially the Psalms.

Benevolent Institutions

More good done often by setting on foot such institutions, than by the utmost personal labor. Benevolent societies should be formed in every congregation, and everyone rich or poor, should feel bound to contribute something. Among the Jews, every man gave. Benevolence elevates feeling and character. The minister should urge all to take part.

Endeavor to have schools in the best order. If the place will allow it, try to have a classical school under your eye; it may raise some boy of genius from obscurity otherwise not reached. Circulating libraries are important under judicious direction. Encourage knowledge; ignorance is always dangerous. Secure the confidence of young men and stir them up to noble interests and pursuits.

The minister should generally enlarge his own library. Have some practical works purposely to lend, in constant circulation. Let your families be a pattern to others.

Expect difficulties from within, as pride, on account of rank, eloquence, learning, authority, sanctity (real or imputed), a worldly spirit, despondency, back sliding; from without, as indifference and opposition, negligence, forgetfulness & c.

There are many encouragements however, and advantages too. He is engaged in the most elevated of all pursuits, and most fitted to enlarge and refine the soul, furnishing the most ample room for doing good. If faithful, he will be loved and honored by all good men, and no affection is stronger than that to a faithful pastor.

Concluding Lecture

Cultivate vital piety in your own soul with all diligence. Labor to be more and more assured about the meaning of the Scriptures. And study the Bible with humility and prayer as little children. Try to be in such a frame and posture as is needed for discerning divine things. Avoid subtle speculations and vain scruples about it.

Be always in such a frame as to be ready to speak on religion. Let your character be, in view of all, *spiritual*. Be anxious to do good to all. Be an example in all things to believers—a light in the world. Grow not careless of improvement. Be careful whom you help to introduce in the ministry. Take a deep and lively interest in the church to which you belong.

- Love your brethren in the ministry.
- Be punctual in attending judicatories.
- Avoid rashness. Be decided—circumspect.
- Be not anxiously careful for the future.
- Widows Fund.
- Roll cares on God.
- Prepare yourself for disappointment. Life in experience differs widely from life in prospect, especially the life of a

Concluding Lecture

minister. Discouragement and temptation beset your whole course.
- Should you come to the conclusion that you have no piety, quit the ministry, or be converted at once.
- Follow conscientiously the leading of Providence.
- Should you change in your creed essentially, do not take advantage of your position in the church to oppose her doctrines: go out openly and honestly from her communion.
- Apparent want of success in a place is not of itself a sufficient reason for leaving it. Work while the day lasts, be it longer or shorter. Engage the pious to pray for you as a minister.
- Keep ever in view your last account.

AMEN!

Bibliography

Selective List of Primary Sources on Church and Ministry By John Williamson Nevin (Chronological)

Addresses Delivered at the Inauguration of Rev. J.W. Nevin, D.D. Chambersburg, Pa.: Publication Office of the German Reformed Church, 1840.

The Ambassador of God: or the True Spirit of the Christian Ministry as Represented in Jesus Christ. Chambersburg, Pa.: Publication Office of the German Reformed Church, 1842.

The Anxious Bench. 2nd ed. Chambersburg, Pa.: Publication Office of the German Reformed Church, 1844.

The Church. Chambersburg, Pa.: Publication Office of the German Reformed Church, 1847.

The Christian Ministry. Chambersburg, Pa.: Publication Office of the German Reformed Church, 1854.

"Service of Ordination and Installation." *Provisional Liturgy.* 1857.

The Mystical Presence, a Vindication of the Reformed or Calvinistic Doctrine of the Holy Eucharist. Philadelphia, 1846. Reprinted, with an Introduction by R. E. Wentz. Hamden, Conn.: Archon Books, 1963.

"Doctrine of the Reformed Church on the Lord's Supper." *The Mercersburg Review* 2 (1850) 421–548.

"Thoughts on the Church." *The Mercersburg Review* 10 (1858) 169–98, 399–426.

"The Old Doctrine of Baptism." *The Mercersburg Review* 12 (1860) 190–215.

The Liturgical Question. Philadelphia, 1862.

Bibliography

"Theology of the New Liturgy." *The Mercersburg Review* 14 (1867) 23–66.
A Vindication of the Revised Liturgy. Philadelphia: J. B. Rodgers, printer, 1867.
"My Own Life." *Weekly Messenger of the German Reformed Church*, February 2, 16; March, 6, 27; April 1870. Reprinted by the Historical Society of the Evangelical and Reformed Church in 1974.
Catholic and Reformed: Selected Theological Writings of John Williamson Nevin. Edited by Charles Yrigoyen Jr. and George H. Bricker. Pittsburgh Original Texts and Translations Series 3. Pittsburgh: Pickwick, 1978.

Nineteenth-Century American Protestantism on the Ministry

Baxter, George A. "Responsibilities of the Ministry and Church." *The American National Preacher* 3 (1828).
Baxter, Richard. *The Reformed Pastor* (1656); reprint ed., Carlisle, Pa.: The Banner of Truth Trust, 1979.
Berry, Philip. "Clerical Culture for the Times." *The Mercersburg Review* 7 (1855) 644.
———. "The Episcopate Viewed as the Centre of Unity." *The Mercersburg Review* 8 (1856) 299.
Bomberger, J. H. A. "Dr. Nevin and His Antagonists." *The Mercersburg Review* 5 (1953) 89–123.
Callender, S. N. "The Apostolic Commission." *The Mercersburg Review* 14 (1864) 325.
Cannon, James Spencer. *Lectures on Pastoral Theology*. New York: Board of publication of the Reformed Protestant Dutch church, 1859.
Child, Frank S. *Colonial Parson of New England*. Gale, 1896.
Clarke, Adam. *The Preacher's Manual*. 1800.
Clarke, James Freeman. "The Revival." *The Monthly Religious Magazine* 19 (1858).
Dorner, J. A. *The Liturgical Conflict in the Reformed Church in North America, with Special Reference to Fundamental Evangelical Doctrines*. Translated by J. H. A. Bomberger. Philadelphia: LOAG, 1868.
Ely, Ezra Stiles. *Visits of Mercy*. 1813.
Finney, Charles. *Lectures on Revivals of Religion*. William G. McLoughlin, ed. Cambridge, Mass.: Belknap, 1960.
Fisher, S. R. "The Moral Dignity of the Ministerial Office." *The Mercersburg Review* 7 (1855) 409–21.
———. "Priestly Element in the Christian Ministry." *The Mercersburg Review* 18 (1866) 114ff.
———. "Qualifications for the Christian Ministry." *The Mercersburg Review* 6 (1854) 423–35.
Gerhart, Emanuel Vogel. "A Devout Ministry." *The Mercersburg Review* 4 (1852) 399–407.

Good, James Isaac. "Are Ministers of the Gospel Priests and Kings?," *Reformed Church Monthly* (February 1868). Reprinted in *The Living Theological Heritage of the United Church of Christ*, edited by Elizabeth C. Nordbeck and Lowell H. Zuck. Cleveland, Ohio: Pilgrim, 1998.

Harbaugh, Henry. "Boardman on Christian Ministry." *The Mercersburg Review* 8 (1856) 1–19.

Harvey, H. *The Pastor: His Qualifications and Duties*. Philadelphia: American Baptist Publication Society,1879.

Heisler, D. Y. "The Apostolic Commission." *The Mercersburg Review* 11 (1859) 337–60.

Helffenstein, Albert. *The Pastor at the Sick Bed*. Philadelphia: Grigg & Elliot, 1836.

Hoppin, James M. *The Office and Work of the Christian Ministry*. New York: Sheldon, 1869.

———. *Pastoral Theology*. New York: Funk and Wagnalls, 1885.

Humphrey, Heman. *Thirty-four Letters to a Son in the Ministry*. 1842.

James, John A. *An Earnest Ministry the Want of the Times*. New York: Dodd, 1848.

Krebs, W. E. "The Christian Minister." *The Mercersburg Review* 15 (1863) 467.

Meade, William. *Lectures on the Pastoral Office*. 1849.

Miller, Samuel. *An Essay on the Warrant, Nature, and Duties of the Office of the Ruling Elders in the Presbyterian Church*. Philadelphia: Presbyterian Board of Publications, 1832.

Murray, Nicholas. *Preachers and Preaching*. New York: Harper & Brothers, 1860.

Order of Worship for the Reformed Church. Philadelphia, 1866.

Peabody, Andrew P. *The Work of the Ministry*. 1850.

Pond, Enoch. *Young Pastor's Guide; or, Lectures on Pastoral Duties*. Bangor: E. F. Duren, 1844.

Porter, T. C. "Address to Congregational Ministers." *The Mercersburg Review* 1 (1849) 515.

Rice, H. L. *Ministerial Qualifications*. Chambersburg, Pa.: J. Pritts, 1836.

Santee, J. W. "New Themes for Protestant Clergy." *The Mercersburg Review* 5 (1853) 577.

Secondary Sources on John Williamson Nevin

Appel, Theodore. *The Life and Work of John Williamson Nevin*. Philadelphia: The Reformed Church Publishing House, 1889.

Bademan, R. Bryan. "Contesting the Evangelical Age: Protestant Challenges To Religious Subjectivity in Antebellum America." Ph.D. dissertation, The University of Notre Dame, 2004.

Barker, Verlyn Lloyd. "John W. Nevin: His Place in American Intellectual Thought." Ph.D. dissertation, St. Louis University, 1970.

Bibliography

Bassett, Joseph. "Eucharist/Liturgical Renewal or John Williamson Nevin on BEM #15." *The New Mercersburg Review* 1 (Autumn 1985) 20–30.

Binkley, Luther J. *The Mercersburg Theology.* Manheim, Pa.: Sentinel, 1953.

Carlough, Williams Leslie. "A Historical Comparison of the Theology of John Williamson Nevin and Contemporary Protestant Sacramentalism." Ph.D. dissertation, New York University, 1961.

———. "A Case Study in Protestant Sacramentalism." *Theology and Life* 7 (1964) 310–18.

Conkin, Paul K. *The Uneasy Center: Reformed Christianity in Antebellum America.* Chapel Hill: University of North Carolina Press, 1995.

Conser, Walter H., Jr. *Church and Confession: Conservative Theologians in Germany, England, and America, 1815–1866.* Macon, Ga.: Mercer University Press, 1984.

Cordoue, John Thomas. "The Ecclesiology of John Williamson Nevin: A Catholic Appraisal." Ph.D. dissertation, The Catholic University of America, 1969.

Cox, Martin, Jr. "To Be the Church: Nevin's Critique of Sectarianism." *The New Mercersburg Review* 3 (Spring 1987) 23–31.

DeBie, Linden. "German Idealism in Protestant Orthodoxy: The Mercersburg Movement, 1840-1860." Ph.D. dissertation, McGill University, 1987.

DiPuccio, William. "The Dynamic Realism of Mercersburg Theology: The Romantic Pursuit of the Ideal in the Actual." Ph.D. dissertation, Marquette University, 1994.

———. *The Interior Sense of Scripture: The Sacred Hermeneutics of John W. Nevin.* Macon, Ga.: Mercer University Press, 1998.

Ebert, Clarence William. "The Liturgical Controversy in the German Reformed Church." Ph.D. dissertation, Temple University, 1959.

Erb, William H., ed. *Dr. Nevin's Theology, Based on Manuscript Class Room Lectures.* Reading: I. M. Beaver, 1913.

Gerrish, B. A. *Tradition and the Modern World: Reformed Theology in the Nineteenth Century.* Chicago: The University of Chicago Press, 1978.

Gilpin, W. Clark. "The Doctrine of the Church in the Thought of Alexander Campbell and John W. Nevin." *Mid-Stream* 19 (October 1980) 417–27.

Hageman, Howard G. "Back to Mercersburg." *Reformed Journal* 35 (August 1985) 5–6.

———. "The Lessons of Mercersburg." *Reformed Journal* 33 (September 1983) 4.

Hambrick-Stowe, Charles. *The Living Theological Heritage of the United Church of Christ Volume 3: Colonial and National Beginnings.* Cleveland: Pilgrim, 1998.

Hamstra, Sam, Jr. "The Americanization of the Church and Its Pastoral Ministry," *The New Mercersburg Review* (Spring, 1992) 3–19.

———. "John Williamson Nevin: The Christian Ministry." Ph.D. dissertation, Marquette University, 1990.

———. "John Williamson Nevin: The Pastoral Office," *The New Mercersburg Review* (Autumn, 1994) 3–23.

Hamstra, Sam, Jr., and Arie J. Griffioen, eds. *Reformed Confessionalism in Nineteenth-Century America: Essays on the Thought of John Williamson Nevin.* Lanham, Md.: Scarecrow, 1995.

Hewitt, Glenn A. *Regeneration and Morality: A Study of Charles Finney, Charles Hodge, John W. Nevin, and Horace Bushnell.* Brooklyn, N.Y.: Carlson, 1991.

Holifield, E. Brooks. "Mercersburg, Princeton, and the South: The Sacramental Controversy in the Nineteenth Century." *Currents in Theology and Mission* 3 (1976) 239–44.

Jones, Charles A., III. "Mercersburg: A Reformed Alternative For the Twentieth Century." *Scholarship, Sacraments and Service: Historical Studies in Protestant Tradition - Essays in Honor of Bard Thompson*, edited by Daniel B. Clendenin and W. David Buschart. Lewiston: Edwin Mellen, 1990.

Josselyn, Lynne. "The Comparative Eucharistic Views of John Wesley and John Nevin." *The New Mercersburg Review* 4 (Autumn 1988) 18–35.

Maxwell, Jack M. *Worship and Reformed Theology: The Liturgical Lessons of Mercersburg.* Pittsburgh: Pickwick, 1976.

Nichols, James Hastings. *The Mercersburg Theology.* New York: Oxford University Press, 1966.

———. *Romanticism In American Theology: Nevin and Schaff At Mercersburg.* Chicago: University of Chicago Press, 1961.

Nordbeck, Elizabeth C. and Lowell H. Zuck. *The Living Theological Heritage of the United Church of Christ Volume 4: Consolidation and Expansion.* Cleveland: Pilgrim, 1999.

Paine, R. Howard. "John Nevin: The Man." *The New Mercersburg Review* 2 (Autumn 1986) 12–16.

Payne, John B. "Nevin and the Sacrament of Baptism." *The New Mercersburg Review* 2 (Autumn 1986) 30–45.

Plummer, Kenneth Moses. "The Theology of John Williamson Nevin in the Mercersburg Period." Ph.D. dissertation, The University of Chicago, 1958.

Richard, George. *History of the Theological Seminary of the Evangelical and Reformed Church at Lancaster, Pennsylvania.* Lancaster, Pa.: Theological Seminary of the Evangelical and Reformed Church, 1952.

Ryan, Francis Patrick. "John Williamson Nevin: The Concept of Church Authority." Ph.D. dissertation, Marquette University, 1968.

Sell, Alan P. F. "J.H.A. Bomberger (1817–1890) versus J.W. Nevin: A Centenary Reappraisal," *The New Mercersburg Review* 8 (Autumn 1990) 3–24.

Shriver, George H. "Passages in Friendship: John W. Nevin to Charles Hodge, 1872." *Journal of Presbyterian History* 58 (Summer 1980) 116–122.

Swander, John I. *The Mercersburg Theology.* Philadelphia: Reformed Church Publication Board, 1909.

Welch, Claude. *Protestant Thought in the Nineteenth Century, Volume I, 1799–1870.* New Haven: Yale University Press, 1972.

Bibliography

Wentz, Richard. *John Williamson Nevin: American Theologian*. New York: Oxford University Press, 1997.
Woolverton, John F. "John Williamson Nevin and the Episcopalians: The Debate on the 'Church Question', 1851–1874." *Historical Magazine* 49 (December 1980) 361–87.
Yrigoyen, Charles, Jr., and George M. Bricker, eds. *Reformed and Catholic: Selected Historical and Theological Writings of Philip Schaff*. Pittsburgh Original Texts and Translations Series 4. Pittsburgh, Pa.: Pickwick, 1979.

www.ingramcontent.com/pod-product-compliance
Lightning Source LLC
Chambersburg PA
CBHW071625170426
43195CB00038B/2125